AF526364

To Dad

from

Kate

Christmas 1978

Parables *of* OLD CATHAY

Books by Paul Eldridge

My First Two Thousand Years
Salome
The Invincible Adam
Prince Pax
If After Every Tempest
Madonna with the Cat
Two Lessons in Love
And Thou Shalt Teach Them
One Man Show
Men and Women
The Intruder
The Bed Remains
Cobwebs and Cosmos
I Bring a Sword
Crown of Empire
Tales of The Fortunate Isles
The Second Life of John Stevens
Seven Against the Night
The Tree of Ignorance
Maxims for a Modern Man
The Homecoming

Parables of OLD CATHAY

Paul Eldridge

South Brunswick and New York: *A. S. Barnes and Co.*
London: *Thomas Yoseloff Ltd*

© 1969 by A. S. Barnes and Co., Inc.
Library of Congress Catalogue Card Number: 78-85662

A. S. Barnes and Co., Inc.
Cranbury, New Jersey 08512

Thomas Yoseloff Ltd
108 New Bond Street
London W1Y OQX, England

SBN: 498 07506 0
Printed in the United States of America

To
SYLVETTE
The Parable Beyond All Time

CONTENTS

Parables *of* OLD CATHAY

Greetings!

From Kong-Fu-Tse, frozen dust
To his countless Lovers, agitated dust:
The difference between the good conduct and the bad
Is the perfumed wind a laughing courtesan
Stirs gently with her jewelled fan from right to left,
And the true and the false are the trembling shadows
Of a candle flickering at an open window.
Drink deeply, then, from your cups of jade,
Have many concubines with small hard breasts
Which crush within your warm, eager hands,
Smoke slowly your long, ivory pipes,
And write faultless poems on lustrous silk
To the river gliding over stones like a white snake,
To the perfect lotus bud; to the immutable pine-tree;
To the wild goose dropping from the tip of his flat beak
Fragile fluttering Spring . . .
But even these do not matter, Lovers of Kong-Fu-Tse . . .

To-Fo . . . . Passé

To-Fo twirls slowly
His long mustaches
Sharp and thin as two pins
And muses:
Today the flower girl looked at you
Serenely
And her breast was still.
Therefore To-Fo, your youth is dead!
Bury it!

Do not carry it about
Roguishly
Like a blue butterfly
Perched
Wings folded
Upon a mandarin's sword.
It is but a stuffed nightingale
With ragged plumes
And an open beak
And its music is only the gold
That rattles in your purse.
Your youth is dead, To-Fo!
Dig a long perpendicular grave
In the center of your heart
And bury it!

Mung Chu Speaks of the Relativity of Things

Li Po sits upon his threshold and meditates—
The buds on the trees have already opened
The stream unwinds and runs like a white steed
Butterflies turn in small circles
Like crowns of invisible monarchs.
"Come forth, Li Po!
Spring is here again, Li Po!"
In Li Po's heart snow is piled mountain-high
Frozen birds fall like small hard twigs
Thin hungry wolves glare with red eyes
While the Wind, the grey Whip, cracks.
"Do not budge, Li Po!
What a terrible winter, Li Po!"
Li Po sits upon his threshold and meditates.

Tsz-Lu Tells His Friend That One May Forgive an Injury, But Cannot Forget It.

The mighty oak
Drops at last
Beneath the blows
Of the dull axe,
But what lightning,
O ancient Friend,
Can cleave
Its shadow
Thinner than the hair
A fledgling carries
In its tightened beak?

Tu Py Explains Why He Tolerates His Querulous Wife

On the peak of my heart
A black-bird perches
Cawing
Ceasclessly—
Should I hurl a rock at its beak
Might I not strike
Myself?

Tu Py's Wife Answers Her Husband's Accusation

I am a black-bird
Cawing
O Tu Py,
Because your love for me
Is as a carcass
Rotting within your heart.
Oh, that your love
Might blossom again
A perfect rose!
I would be a tiny nightingale
Perched upon your lips
More lightly than a petal
Singing golden praises
To Tu Py,
Prince of Men!

Wung Po Believes in Reincarnation Due to the Change That Has Taken Place in His Wife

I married a lamb—
The lamb died—
A ferocious tigress
Is sharing my bed.

Tsi Ouan Wishes to Believe in Immortality

The leaves of the lotus-flower
Fall into the River
Which flows from the Great Mountain
Into the White Sea.

Some say
The River will change its manner
Will flow out of the White Sea
Upward
Over the Great Mountain
Bringing back
The leaves of the lotus-flower.
I drink a thousand cups of wine
Hoping to understand this.

Su T'chu Writes to His Teacher About His Accomplishment

I have climbed upward,
On and on,
As you have taught me,
O beloved Master.
I have reached the ultimate peak
Of the smooth perpendicular
Mountain of Nothingness.

Sing Po Meditates on Universal Brotherhood

Walking slowly through the garden
His hands hidden in the wide sleeves
Of his gold-embroidered gown
Sing Po, Lama of Buddah the Conqueror,
Meditates rapturously
On the universal brotherhood
Of all living things,

Crushing the while
Underneath his slippers of brocaded silk
Caterpillars pulsing with the wings of butterflies
And ants, architects of round-topped pyramids,
And tearing with the edge of his hem
A spider's web
On which the dew-drops lie softly
Like precious stones without weight.

Chang Wang Presents the Reckoning to his Beloved

Who was the faithful one,
You,
Who wound your lovely body
In Virtue's glacial cloak,
But like some lost somnambulist
Wandered, desolate
Among dreams of other loves?
Or I,
Who dizzied with passion
Pressed other breasts against my own
And slaked my thirst at other lips,
But who, like some solitary monk
Turning ceaselessly his prayer-wheel,
Always finds his God,
Dreamed only of you?
Who was the faithful one, Beloved?

Lung Mo Bemoans the Transitoriness of Fame

The small silken parasol
Of my wife
Eclipses the glory of the Sun,
Think, O Sing Hai,
What trifle can eclipse
The glory of our fame!

Ti Pi Rebukes a Vulgar Crowd

At noon
When Ti Pi awoke
In the puddle
Which faces the Old Celestial wineshop
He played long
And tenderly
With the golden rays
That danced upon his sleeves:
"O perfect eye of Truth
Thou alone discernest
The priceless jewel
Though it lies in the mud!"

Wung Ouan, Traveler in the Night

Wung Ouan carried a lighted lantern
Even when the sun was overhead,
Saying that the evil thoughts of men
Made perennial night.

Sing Po, Mystic, Expounds the Mystery of Body and Soul

In the upper branches
Of the tree
Which grows
On the edge of the lake
Birds swing;
In its lower branches
Fish swim;
And the moon
Sleeps
Upon both.

Emperor T'ang, Skeptic

Closer than my body's shadow,
Follows the blind Nameless One,
Carrying in his tightened fist
Time, the thin spluttering Candle,
And in his swollen Cheeks
Death, the grey Wind—
So fill and refill my deep, golden horn
With the strongest wine,
O wise men of Cathay,
Before declaiming in magnificent verse
My immortality,
That I may nod,
My eyes heavy with dreams
And believe.

Ku Mung Mourns the Passing of his Years

The rose is dangling
On its broken stem,
Its petals are dropping
One by one—
Who shall gather them together
To make a rose again?

Chu Teh Calls From Outre-Tombe

Life was a weary trudging
Through sticky mud—
I yearned for Death,
The Golden Wind,
The Merger of Things—
I thought I would join the cosmos
In her rapturous swing,
Dance with the stars,
Kiss the red lips of moons,
Scatter voluptuous perfume
From a rose's chalice.

Are the cracks
In this mouldy wood
The dancing stars?
Are these red worms
Crawling
Heavily
Like pregnant things
Upon my mouth
The lips of moons?

Is my coffin the cosmos
In her rapturous swing?
Enlighten me,
O Gautama Siddhartha,
Holiest of Buddahs!

Tsang Ch'ing Writes to His Friend About the State of His Health

My heart is an old horse
Dragging his heavy load
In faithful submission—
Alas!
He is growing weary,
He will stumble
And fall!

Li Fu's Double Mourning

The things I loved died—
I dug a grave
And buried them
With all the pomp
Of tears and verse.

"I shall return in the Spring
And gather daisies
The gentle souls
Of the things I loved."

In the Spring
I returned
And found upon the grave
Of the things I loved
A dead rat
And stout, angry flies
Devouring him.

T'ang To Answers His Old Pupil

The meaning of happiness, beloved To Lung?
A large-holed sieve
Dipped into a basin of water
Seems full,
But raise it—
Only a few trembling drops
Hang a while to its bottom
And make it rust.
Therefore what answer shall I give?
I am old.
I do not ask the meaning of things.
I built me out of two small trees
That the lightning struck,
Serenely and without compunction
A comfortable coffin.
Upon the polished lid
I wrote in large perfect letters:
"Well, T'ang To?
No matter, T'ang To!"
With two broken branches
I beat upon it many fine tunes—

To my first love
To the joy of virtue
To Truth's imperishable Sovereignty—
The sound is always hollow
So that I cannot tell
Whether Life answers me
Or Death
Or both together.

I smoke the fine long pipe you sent me
And sip slowly my bad wine,
When I grow tipsy
The Moon dances in a silken robe
Like my first love . . .

Tang Si Believes that Clothes Make the Emperor

Lung Chin's cat
Seeing the stuffed skin
Of my dog
Humped her back,
Unsheathed her claws
And spat.

Yen Yu Describes His Weariness of Life

An ant
Tumbling into his cell
The last load
Dropping from his mouth.

Lin Piao Mourns the Futility of Man's Life

Across the Desert Eternity
Our years are trudging—
Swollen-kneed Camels
Loaded with sacks of dead days,
Seeking water.

Teng Hsiao Replies to a Friend Who Complains About Those in Power and Suggests a Remedy

Do not famished wolves
Tear the throats
Of shivering lambs?
And do not packs
Of powerful hounds
Tear the throats
Of howling wolves?

Ghen Si Fu Ridicules the Vanity of Certain Statesmen

The ant bore its thin way
Underneath the small rock
That stands in the Imperial Forest—
Thereafter it called itself
"Carrier of mighty mountains
Pillar stupendous of the Great Empire."

Fo Ghen Says That People Should Not Blame One Another, But the God of Many Faces, Fountain of All Evil

The trembling bird
Seeing his favorite leaves
Scattered on the ground
And driven by the winds
Calls the naked tree
A cruel parent
And a host lacking in politeness.

The tree
Watching the bird fly
To distant warmer lands
Calls after him
Beating branch against branch:
"Ungrateful guest!
Brother to the many-legged worm
And the greedy ant!"

Hung Ma Explains Why He Suspects Good People

The tail-less fox
Moves warily
Through the grasses
Having learned
The meaning
Of good traps.

Wung Lo Consoles His Friend in His Nightmarish Trouble

You open your eyes,
O Kung-si Hwa,
And the wild tiger
That tore at your entrails
Was but your hand
Pressing against your heart
As if making
An amorous pledge.

Shuh-Ts'i Explains Himself and His Thoughts

I am a still round lake
Hidden among tall, melancholy mountains,
And my thoughts, long-necked swans,
Glide smoothly
In circles
Forming a lucent moon,
But their shadows are black serpents
Devouring them—
Their agony is resigned and silent
Like the weary agony of a dying moon.

Mi Lung's False Messenger

Night is not the Black Pigeon
Knocking gently
At my lady's window,
Cooing
"It is time for love!"

Night is the Black Dagger
Piercing the heart
Of the lonesome one.

Bing Tu Disagrees With Those Who Bewail the Brevity of Life and the Eternity of Death

Finding pain the sole measure of time
Bing Tu considers Life longer
Than the Foamy River
Which runs from one end of the Earth
To the other,
And Death the quick drooping
Of a weary eyelid.

Bing Lo Answers Wung Tchi Fung, Who Reprimands Him for His Lack of Ambition

Bing Li placed his soft hands
Over his large belly
And asked, smiling:
"Has Death
Been banished from the Earth,
O Wung Tchi Fung?"

Quam Tsi T'ung Finds Violence Weaker Than Serenity

The moth
Enraged
Beats against the lamp
His wings forming
Countless tiny fans
And falls at last
A fragile pinch of grey ashes.
The lamp burns on
Tranquilly.

Ti Chi's Delusion

I thought you were
A deep cool lake—
I plunged
And drowned
In slimy mud.

Tsi-Tu Contradicts the Notion That Goodness Is Beauty and Beauty Goodness

Mun-T'si,
The farmer,
Found the weeds
That he plucked
And burned
Often more beautiful
Than the plants
He had nurtured
With so much care.

Doctor Ming Tsu Distrusts the Over-Solicitous

The bitterer the drug
I prescribe
The thicker the coating
Of honey.

Ling-Tu Chides the Would-Be Poets

The worm listens
To the humming of the bee
And thinks what greater wonders
He could tell
The radiant roses
If he could hum—
Or roses understood
The tongue of silence.

Two Opinions

You regret
That memory is a tiny cup
So soon overbrimming.
Ah, Tung Lung,
Would that the tiny cup
Were deeply cracked
Retaining nothing!

Tsi Chung Witnesses a Resurrection

Within the cavernous
Shadow-filled orbits
Of a saint's skull
Unearthed by the greedy snouts
Of hungry jackals
Two fireflies
Startled
Beat in terror
Their lucent wings.

She She-Ye Challenges Life

Life—
You are an idiot goose
A garland of roses about your neck
A cherry in your beak—
I shall pierce you
With a long silver spit
And broil you
With punctilious care
Over corals ablaze—
I shall consume you
With unequalled relish
Smacking my lips
In loud content.
Your sharp, brown bones
The final memory of you,
I shall throw with bravado
To Time, the big-jawed Mastiff—
He will crunch them
And swallow them
Utterly—
Alas!

Kü Pih-You Meditates on Creation

Each thing I own
Slowly turns to dust,
When I am dead
I shall bequeath
To my descendants
A tall mountain.
Did thus the dead God
Create the Earth
He bequeathed to Man?

Tsang Si, Once Laureled Poet, Explains Why He Is no Longer Ambitious

The Valley
Like a snake
Whose belly is filled
With many rats
Unrolled and dozing
Under the cool shadow
Of the hill
Thinks
And the thoughts
Move gently
Over the grasses:
"The hill is young,
It reaches for the stars,
Its arm will weary,
It will crumble,
It, too, will become
A valley
Dozing—"

Li Ting-Yi Tells About his Experience at the Bier of His Father

So still is death—
A breath drawn
Is the wind
Howling
Over wild waters.
So still is death—
The heart pulsing
Is a hammer
Pounding on an iron gate.
So still is death—
A thought rising
Is an owl hooting
In an empty nest.
So still is death—
A tear dropped
Is a stone
Hurtling
Against shattered glass—
So still is death.

Chin Li Ridicules the Poets Who Claim That Poetry Is Only a Matter of Form not of Substance

Tse-Kung's dog barked
The whole night
Desperately,
His head in the air,
Though no one passed
And the Moon hid
In the scabbard of the clouds.
The sleepless neighbors
Stoned him to death.

To One Who Assuming Postures of Profound Meditation Considers Himself a Great Philosopher

Ping Sy's tomcat
Squats for long hours
Upon his master's window-sill
His head bent upon his soft chest
His eyes forming two oblique
Luminous lines—
His thoughts
Are endless files
Of timid brown mice
And vast circles
Of absent-minded swallows
Whose wings like toy fans
Beat vaguely the white dust.

Wung Mi Considers the Cosmos a Toy in the Hands of a Divinity and Tells How Simple It Is to Achieve It

The small hand of my beloved
Shakes
Playfully
Her ivory fan
With many inscriptions
And Autumn,
Sad Knight of the Dead Flowers,
Appears
Riding on his white steed.

Hu Pen Wu, Professor of Letters, Explains the Tragedy of Comedy and the Comedy of Tragedy

The wind laughs
The green leaves shiver
And drop—
The wind whistles
The funeral march
The withered leaves
Rush ahead
Cymbals of laughter.

Huang Wang—To One Who Is Proud That He Never Changes His Opinions

The mouth
Of the gargoyle
Through which the rain
Does not flow,
O Tung-Chi,
Is choked
With sand and mud
And infested
With vermin.

Su Wen-Mao Explains Why One Feels Most Alone in Crowds

In the tumult
Of the noon-sun
Each leaf
In the forest
Dazzles
Like a knife
Newly sharpened.

Pang Chu Considers his Life

I ride
A wooden stallion
In a merry-go-round
That turns
And turns
To grotesque
And dreary music . . .
I shall grow dizzy
And fall off.

Tsu Lung Makes an Error

At first
I believed
It was the full moon
That followed me
As I crossed
The long wooden bridge
Which spans the river
Between Tsu and Ch'in,
And in pride
I said:
"The moon is my shadow."

Later
I saw
It was but a cloud
Chased by the wind
And in abasement
I muttered:
"I am the shadow
Of a cloud."

To Fo Bargains With Divinity

The tortured grape
Bleeds
And there is wine,
But To Fo's many sorrows
And endless torment
Only bring forth groans and lamentations
Annoying his patient friends
And ruffling the placid air
That should rise and touch Heaven
Smoothly
Like the soft finger-tips
Of a young Empress.
O Lord of Things
Master Economist
Gatherer of stray shadows
And forgotten hours,
Why continue this useless extravagance,
This profligate waste?
Shower upon To Fo
Many joys and much pleasure
He will smile
Serenely
With lengthened lips
And half-closed eyes
He will make less noise
Than a young timid mouse
Testing the new entrance
To a sweetly-odored cupboard.

Tsz-Káu Relates the Fable of Immortality

When Autumn,
Red Emperor of the Chase,
Gallops
Through forest and field
Hounds howling
Arrows shrieking,
The Trees,
Ancient hives
Of terror-stricken leaves,
Speak:
"Fear not,
O children of our boughs,
But rejoice,
For Wind,
The White Gardener,
Gathers you
In his great arms
To the Land of Eternal Spring,
Where he hangs you
One by one
Upon the immortal branches
Of the Golden Tree,
And you shall blossom
Resplendent
Forever,
O children of our boughs!"

Judge Chen-Po-Ta Finds It Difficult to Pronounce Judgment

The glowing beak
Of the swooping bird
Cut like a sharp knife
The hairy caterpillar
That devoured the bark of the tree;
The cat pounced upon the bird
Scattering to the wind
Its torn feathers;
Ling Mo's mastiff
Strangled the cat,
Lapping its blood—
Should the mastiff
Wagging his tail
Joyously
At the approach of his owner,
Be clubbed to death?
Answer,
O Kong-Fu-Tse,
Wisest of Judges,
Master divine
Of the Proper Conduct?

Ling Yu, Astronomer, Sits at His Table Computing the Cosmic Formula

Tonight
The Moon is a bucket of milk
The Immortal Maid,
Absent-minded,

Dreaming of her Lover
The dazzling Sun
Spills upon the Earth—
My fingers are wet
My ink is white.

The Punishment of Chu-Min, Philosopher

He thought
And thought
And thought
Until the Earth
Became a shimmering spark
And Heaven
A frozen tear
And he vanished
On the puff of a wind.

Tsz-Káu Warns the Poor of the Charity of the Rich

In the Winter
The trees are mendicants
Lifting crooked hands
In supplication.
The gods are bountiful—
They throw upon them
Profusely
Sleet and snow.

Tao Chu Ridicules the Sentimentality of the Classic Poets

You are wandering,
O Tsz-chang,
Friend of my youth,
A weary exile
Among cruel strangers—
Thinking of your misfortune
I drink deeply and often,
And the wine
Mingling with your image
Tastes rich and fragrant
As if drawn
From the imperial cellar.

Wung Po Tchi, Poet, Admonishes a Princess Who Rejects Him Because of His Low Birth

The rose
Whose sweet perfume
Makes you open your nostrils
And lower
Slowly
Your fine long lashes
Is but the daughter
Of manure
O Perfect Princess—
Tear it
And throw it away!

Mi To Belittles the Value of Glory

The mighty general, Tu Ku,
Returning from the conquest
Of rebellious provinces
Found his wide silken slippers
A greater pleasure
Than the twenty medals
Imbedded with precious gems
That the grateful Emperor
Had pinned upon his chest.

Ki K'ang Speaks of the Mischievous Tricks of Time

At first
Wung Mi's wife
Waited for him
At the corner
Of the road
Turning her head
Anxiously
At the faintest noise.

Later,
She sat on the doorstep
Of her home
Her hands upon her lap
Gazing in one direction.

Finding it tiresome
She remained
At the open window
Her eyes fixed
Upon her sewing.

Now
Wung Mi must call
Several times
Before his wife,
Gossiping with her neighbors,
Hears him.

To Fung Tse Teaches His Pupils Irreverence for the Gods

How simple,
My Children,
To be the Creator
Of a Universe!
Drop into a pot
Of hot water
A lump of grease.
Upon the agitated Firmament
Shall appear
A thousand glittering Stars,
Long Milky Ways
With pointed tails,
Golden Suns
With multitudinous Earths
Dancing about them
The mad dance of Time,
Pallid crumbling Moons
Clinging
Desperately
For one instant
Onto the rim,
Then
Falling
Falling
Through the Great Tumultuousness
Of Infinity . . .

Yu Hung-Chang, Dramatist of the Imperial Court, Presents Hamlet of the Orchard

Whether,
While drowned
In perfumed sleep,
A timorous Blossom
Kissed by the rapturous mouths
Of Sun and Moon
And rocked in merry lullabies
By silver-fingered breezes
To drop
To pulse
O'er the Vast Void
In frenzied terror
One instant
And be no more—
Or,
At death of Summer
Aglow
And heavy-seeded
Awaken
An Apple
The jester's bell
Of pompous Wind
The rattle drum
Of petulant Rain
The tortured banquet hall
Of slimy, gluttonous Worm—
O mighty God of Life
O myriad-armed Tree
Answer!

Yen-Yu Deplores the Illusion of Youth

In the Summer
Earth
The Old Harlot
Hides her centuries
Of lust and vice
Beneath a gorgeous dress
Of daffodils and buttercups
And dazzling grasses.
For her hair she tumbles
Cataracts of red roses,
She enamels with lilies
Her face torn and bitten
By raping hurricanes,
She sprinkles on her bosom
Showers of perfume.
The young birds enamored
Believe her a virgin
And serenade her
With rapturous melodies.
Earth
The Old Harlot
Laughs
And her laughter
Is the mocking Wind.

Ming Lo Writes Two Epitaphs

ON A FLY

After a long season
Of cheerful buzzing
And profitable biting
I alighted
Upon a lump of sugar
And on the bed of sweetness
I fell asleep.
Mules and men
Worn with labor
And eager for just rewards
Stop and ponder!

ON THE MELTING SNOW

I was the symbol
Of magnificence.
Gaze upon me
Earth's vain ones
And weep!

Tu Fung Shi Counsels His Friend Not to Be Upset by His Critics

The blind man
Shouted in the market-place
At high noon:
"The sun is dead!
Night has devoured the sun!"
Should the sun,
O Kung Li,
My ancient friend,
Drop into the Great River
Like a stricken bird?

Peh-I Speaks of the Folly of Worry

The mushroom
Devoured by ants
Asks, disconsolate:
"What shall become of me
When the oak
Whose shadow I break
With my whiteness
Is felled
By the great axe
Of the Clouds?"

Li Pe Explains the Difference in Time by the Difference in Space

In my youth
I turned
Breathless
At every corner
Of the Thousand Streets
Expecting
Marvellous encounters.

Now
I walk
The Long Unbended Path
Slowly
Eyes half-shut
Expecting Nothing.

Why Chin Su Has Become a Drunkard

My heart is a cave
Dark and cool,
But within it I keep
Flasks of rarest wines—
I invited my friends
To come and drink with me
And make merry—
Alas!
They entered half-way,
But scared
Rushed out—
I must drink alone.

Mao-Tse Regrets His Prudence

My soul was a conflagration—
Alarmed
I poured water
Ceaselessly—
My soul is a hcap of ashes,
Thin threads of smoke
Curl in the wind
And shape themselves
Into laughing mouths.

Sing Lo's Warning to His Beloved

Time,
O Chiang Ching,
Is a mocking sprite
Carrying
A big wet sponge—
Bolt your heart,
Hang upon its gate
Silver bars
And golden locks
And stud them
With long diamond spikes—
Leave not a crevice
A hair's breadth
Unsealed securely,
For Time
Watches
In the shadow of a pulse
And his wet sponge
Would wash away
My image
From your heart,
O Beloved!

Tan Lien-Chang Warns the Vainglorious

A rose of unusual hue and scent
Her summer's day upon her praises spent—
The inflaming essence of the field's perfume
She vowed Creation did consume
To shape her breast. And from the sunken Sun
Distilled the fabric of her dress was spun,
While breezes and the birds were here
To sing her charms to the dazzled Sphere.

Alas! The wind her head did bend
And now she did behold the other end.
"O God, what shame is this, what wrong!
My being rests within the dung!
Tear me out! How canst Thou bear
O Lord, such root for one so fair?"

The answer to her wish she promptly got—
That very evening she was cut,
And being fresh of scent and bright of color
Was directly brought into the parlor
And placed within a crystal vase
Released forever from her vast disgrace.

Alas! Ere the aureate Moon her eye did close
Icy and anguished grew the heart of the rose,
Forlorn, she moaned: "Manure! Manure!"
In vain that godly balsam to conjure.

Now her corpse sans scent sans hue lies outspread
For mounds of dust a shifting bed.

Duke of Lu Speaks of Grandeur and Death

Autumn
Knight of the Sorrowful Visage
Scattered his bounty—
Filled the bellies of fruits
With honey
And the hearts of plants
With savor—
The stalks of corn he gilded
And plumed
Like armies of princes
On parade
And the leaves of trees
He sprinkled
With his blood.
Now
Pale and haggard
His lance broken
And his armor shredded
He awaits
Impassive
The mortal thrust
Of the Knight of the Burning Ice.
The wind will entomb
His mangled corpse
Beneath the shifting mounds
Of clattering leaves
And sweep it
Over the black cataract
Of Dead Years.

Tschiu-Sy Tells a Young Artist That It Is Foolish to Expect Others to Partake in the Joy of His Successes

Ming Gu, the young general,
Returning from many conquests,
Rode in triumph
Toward the Imperial Palace.
Ku Chin, the ancient farmer,
Bending over the spade
With which he dug
His miserable garden,
Coughed, exclaiming angrily
And spitting:
"What dust!"

Fu Lung, Politician, Explains Himself

The one-skinned mouse
Hangs from the teeth of the cat
Tail outward.
The many-colored chameleon
Escapes the cruel claws
Of the bewildered eagle.
Fu Lung is humble and obedient
He follows always
The incomparable precepts
Of the Omniscient Master
Creator of all things.

Old Bing Lin Pities Youth's Illusion of Permanence

Every Spring
The new leaves
Upon the trees
In the forest
Challenge the Wind
Laughing:
"Blow
Big Mouth
Blow
Until your cheeks split!
Blow
Big Mouth
Blow!"

Li Chung Is Rejected by a Lady

I am a dried well,
Smothered by black shadows,
You are a glowing moon,
Li Chung,
Seeking in vain
To find reflection there.

Lin Mi Praises Modesty

Let the vain bird
Sing to all the winds
His vulgar love—
The love of butterfly

Would wither
Shamed
If the gentle rose
Heard the flutter of his wings.

Bing Li Tells Why He Refused to Lend Money

Returning from my trip
To the White Mountain
I discovered that the road
I had taken in the morning
Had lengthened considerably.

Ti Lu Explains Ghosts

Withered leaves
The wind rolls on
Scaring the sparrows
That rocked on them.

Chung-Kung Ridicules the Poets Who Always Invoke the Stars

Their palms are callous
From applause,
Their throats are hoarse
From exclamation,
O eternal Stars—
Stop your rapturous dances
And bow to them
In gratitude!

Peng Chen Watches a Girl Passing by His Door

Pray that I live long
O passing maiden,
Pray that my memory
Remain clear and strong,
So shall your youth
And your beauty last,
Treasured as radiant jewels
Mocking the evil years.

Ming Fu Laughs at Si Tsu, Who, Unappreciated, Is Certain That the Future Generations Will Understand Him and Glorify Him

The Future,
O learned Si Tsu,
Is a large mouth
Wide open
Laughing uproariously
At the Past.

Han Po Says It Is Often Better to Avoid Old Friends

To the legless worm
The magnificent butterfly
Is still but a caterpillar
On false wings.

Ti Pu, Poet of Disillusion, Claims That People Do Not Distinguish Between True Art and Its Vulgar Imitations

At midnight
Mi Tchi, the diligent farmer,
Lit the small lantern
That swung gently
From a rope—
The pompous cock
Flapped his great wings
Like an emperor's precious fan
And crowed triumphantly
The ancient hymn
To the rising Sun!

Hoang-Ti Describes the Loneliness of Old Age

All the leaves
Have dropped
Save one
Crumpled
On the tip
Of the sapless twig
Clattering
In terror
At the howling
Of the winds.

Houng Su Explains Why He No Longer Writes Poetry

Your love, Cui Ping,
Overbrims my heart,
The Bird of Song
Is drowned.

Yu-Chung's Masterpiece

His eyes tightly shut
Yu-Chung, famous author
Of a thousand poems,
Drew circles
With a dry brush
Upon a sheet of black silk,
Saying:
"At last I am writing the Truth!"

Prince Fi-Tu, Exile

The great black log
On which I sit
Is devoured by ravenous ants
While I am devoured
By ravenous regrets.
The great black log is still
And I never stir.
Why should we clamor
Like toothless winds:
"I was a mighty oak tree!
I was a famous prince!"

Pin Fo Complains Against Misinterpretation

In the sand of my life
I draw mystic lines and circles
With an ivory cane
Explaining the meaning of me—
Feet and hoofs step upon them
Distorting their shapes.

Lian Chao Chi Rebukes Those Who Believe They Have Discovered Truth

Chin Suy filled
Feverishly
His small leather bag
With the white sand
That soothes the vast anger
Of the Blue Sea,
And shouted,
Triumphant:
"I have captured
The measureless shore
Of the limitless waters,
O people of Cathay!"

Shan-Lien Finds the Attainable Uninteresting

You were a steep mountain
With peaks of blinding snow
Freezing the long lashes
Of the rising sun.
Now that I have reached the top
Nothing seems easier
Than climbing mountains
With peaks of blinding snow.
Now I am crawling
For the stars.

Wu T'ang Changes His Mind

I wrote upon a leaf of silk:
"The water-lily glows a while
On the peak of its green, hard stem,
Then glides
Gently
Upon the breast of the river
Forever.
How pleasant to be a water-lily!
Man is like a water-lily!"

Yesterday
I saw upon the shore of the river
A thousand withered water-lilies
Rotting in the sands.

Today
I write upon a leaf of silk:
"The water-lily glows a while
On the peak of its green, hard stem,
Then rots
Upon the sands
Of the shore.
How sad to be a water-lily!
Man is like a water-lily!"

Sing-Lu Speaks of Memories in Old Age

In the Winter
The sleepy Earth
Draws over her wrinkled face
The soft, white quilt,
And dreams
Blue and yellow daisies.

Ouan Yi Criticizes the Poets Who, Having Nothing to Say, Hide the Vacuum in a Difficult Style

The spider weaves intricate webs
To capture a fly
But the Moon captures the Earth
With a simple net of white silver.

Hsu Tang Says That Often a Work Which the Artist Considers of No Importance Is the Only Thing Which Survives Him and Constitutes His Glory

In the Autumn,
Of Chu Ming's beautiful garden
Nothing remained intact
Save one small violet
Shivering in the bark of a tree.
Neighbors exclaimed:
"A fragment of an impeccable Sky
Fallen to the Earth!"

Yang Kai-Hue Ridicules Foolish Piety

Blessed be Thou
Fu-Sang
Tree of Immortality
And God of All the Forests
For casting Thy black shadow
Upon me, humble shrub,
Smothering me!

Lu Mi Tells the People to Mistrust Politicians of All Factions

The worm has many rings
But one mouth
That devours.

Chin Tu Fears a Revolution

The dust lies submissive and still
Underneath our feet,
But when the Wind,
The mad, blind Horseman,
Gallops through the country
His long white claws
Pluck our half-closed eyes
And stifle our gasping breaths.

Ouan Si, Mathematician, Disputes the Science of Numbers

Having discovered that ceaseless labor
Plus perennial disillusion
Equal a bowl of soggy rice
And a cup of unpalatable tea,
Ouan Si, former student of Mathematics,
Considers the problems he solved in his youth
Vain concoctions of vainer minds.

Cheng Wang Evaluates Things and Man

The buds stud the trees
The grasses crack the earth
The frogs unstiffened leap
The things of dust live again
But the dead we loved rot on.

The song gurgles in the throats of birds
The brooks rehearse their never-ending tale
The crickets half asleep atune their legs
The things of dust live again
But the dead we loved rot on.

Thus year by year the Spring shall come
The things of dust will live again
But the dead we loved will rot on and on.

Tsuy Hi Ko Writes to One Who Yearns to Achieve

The top-most star
Upon the ultimate peak
Of the Great Circumference
Blinks in hopeless ennui.

The Young Empress Is Bored

The peacock struts solemnly
In the Great Imperial Garden
And his shadow passes slowly
Over the wide fountain whose waters
Are a perfect counterpart of Heaven.

The young Empress sitting at the open window
Sighs:
"Whatever the magnificence of the colors
The shadow must always be black."

Tu Pi Ouan, Geometrician, Explains That All Things Are Parallel and Meet Long Before Infinity

Sitting upon the wall
That surrounds his small garden,
And fanning his face with a large bamboo leaf,
Hun Hi found himself
On a parallel line
With the peak of the Brown Mountain
Which is covered with snow
The four seasons of the year.

Tung Tchi Sy Speaks of the Finality of Death

Drop a stone into the sea,
O hopeful people,
When shall it cast
Its reflection
Upward
Upon the shore?

Ki Tsz-Jen Sums It Up

The fretful flies
Buzz furiously
And strike their heads
Against the window-pane,
Those within the room
And those without
Seeking safety,
But Master Hour
Who crumbles flies
With his subtle finger-tips
And scatters their dust
In the Wind
Holds Court
Both within
And without.

Two Subtle Philosophers

The subtle Tung Mi
Advised his disciples
To weep in joy
And laugh in sorrow
Thus outwitting Pain,
Goddess of sharp teeth
And long claws.
Sing Po,
Subtler than his master,
Neither laughed nor wept,
Being unable to distinguish
Between joy and sorrow.

Si Po Puts His Grandchild to Sleep

Having read the ten thousand masterpieces
Constituting the complete wisdom of mankind,
Si Po puts his grandchild to sleep
Recounting the beautiful legend
Of the Great Storm in which not a leaf stirred
And the Famous Flood which could not drown
The tiniest kitten.

Fang Tu Explains to a Bookworm the Futility of Knowledge

Mass shadow upon black shadow,
O learned Tai,
Shall they ever rise
Majestic
Like the Tall Mountain
That watches
The round waters
Of the Yellow Lake?
Shall they ever press
More heavily
Earth's patient face
Than the ruffled feather
A fledgling drops?

Sy Mo Speaks of the Eccentricities of Fate

Because of her great modesty
The beautiful daughter
Of Ming T'ang
The Magnificent Emperor
Locked herself in her room
And refused to marry.
Her body lies exposed
To the vulgar crowd
Of an ill-famed museum
Of a far-away country.
The brass tablet
Upon her breast
Reads:
"A famous Courtesan
Of the First Dynasty."

Kung Chao-Fu, Exiled Governor, Compares Himself to the Shell on the Shore of the River Yeh, Where He Sits and Broods

The River flows
On and on
Bearing all things
Save me
For the tide
Has flung me
Upon the shore
And filled me
With worms
And mud—
The River flows
On and on . . .

T'ung Kung's Challenge

I accuse the leprous sky
Devoured by the giant vermin
Sun and Moon and Stars
Liars and deceivers
Enchainers of Truth,
I shall nail across its face
A vast black cloud
Leaden and impenetrable,
And in the thick circular darkness
In the frozen immovable silence
I shall shatter and fling
The ponderous shackles
Of the sole and perfect God.

Old Fan Ch'i Makes His Last Calculation on the Abacus

I cupped my hands
To gather life
But my hands were sieves
And life was water.

My hands are rust
Studded and gnawed
By grains of sand—
The final sum.

Lo T'ang Li, Ascetic

When alive
The soul of Lo T'ang Li
Climbed his thin bent body
Swiftly
Softly
Like a small white squirrel
Stepping over fragile moons
Cracking them
Like thin dry twigs
And dropping across Eternity
As unpalatable nuts
Multitudinous blue and yellow stars
Until dazzling
Estatic
It attained last Heaven's uttermost peak.
There
Squatting securely
Among the incomparable gods of China
It discussed
With ultimate assurance
The meaning of the true and the false
Declaiming passionately
Against the useless and degrading burden
Of the human flesh . . .
When dead
The soul of Lo T'ang Li,

A thin grey breath
Made one faint, headless wavelet
And mingled thereafter
Forever
With the formless intangible air
Which men and dogs inhale
Unconscious
And birds and silk-spun butterflies
Beat their wings against
In disdainful mastery.

Na-Kung Kwoh, Young Poet, Laments His Condition

Why am I sad
When the sun shines
And the air is filled
With the perfume of flowers?

Why is my heart leaden
When Nature makes merry
And hill and valley
Reecho with her laughter?

Why am I as one dead
When the world is reborn
And each thing proclaims
Its immortality?

Alas, why am I man
When there are trees and brooks
And songs pour forth
From the throats of birds?

Tschi Fu Speaks on the Meaning of Cause and Effect

The lamb
White and tender
As a tamed pigeon
Vaunted his innocence,
Complaining bitterly
Against the ceaseless cruelty
Of wolves and foxes—
Ganesha, God of Wisdom,
Smiled
His eyes closing
Slowly
Lashes touching the tips of lashes:
"What small teeth you have
O melancholy lamb!"

Chou Chang Advises Practicality to a Poet

The stars are radiant queens
Walking majestically across Infinity,
But the edges of their azure cloaks
Trail in the muddy pools of the Earth.

Lo Foh, Harlot, Invites Pih-Yu, Young Poet

Come to me, Pih-yu!
Place your head upon my bosom
And I shall cover you with my silken shawl,
You shall hear the beating of my heart
And breathe the perfume of my body,
There shall be utter silence
And utter peace
Nothing I ask of you
Nay, not even the mock promise
Of eternity.
My love shall be of a day
Of an hour perhaps
But all blossom
Like the scarlet rose
In its outburst of glory.
You shall fear no decay
No withering kiss,
No sigh shall pull at your sleeve
No tear shall trip your feet,
You shall drink of my beauty
Without reproach
And without regret
And with the joy of me
Still in your heart
And the perfume of me
Still upon your lips
You shall leave me—
Come to me, Pih-yu!

The Miracle of Ming Lu, Poet, and His Reward

The Emperor commanded:
"Go plant roses
In the desert,
Ming Lu!"
And the Court laughed.

Ming Lu planted roses
In the desert
Watered them with his tears
And cooled them with his breath—
In the Spring
There were roses white as the moon
And roses red as the setting sun
And roses yellow as the sands.
And the desert was a garden,
The gift of Ming Lu, Poet,
To the people of Cathay.

And the Emperor commanded:
"Let Ming Lu be stoned!"
And the Court laughed.

Chu-Mi Pities the Optimism of Old Age

The black log
Rotting on the hillock
Of manure
Is awaiting the advent of Spring
And the return of the nightingale

That sang one evening
Amid the dazzling leaves
Of its branches
Gracefully spread
Like the candelabrum
Of the Sacred Temple.

Li Hung Chang Finds the Division of the Year Into Four Seasons No Longer Valid

It is always Winter
For have not my hopes
Which were blossoming trees
Dropped all their leaves,
And has not the wind
Wound about their shrivelled limbs
Shrouds of ice?
And in my heart
Does not the red-eyed hyena
Laugh?

Syu Wu Tells Why He Stopped Studying Philosophy Just Before Receiving His Degree

Every door I opened
In the spacious Castle of Knowledge
Showed me an empty room.
Thus, having learned wisdom,
I left the last one
Tightly locked.

To One Who Is Enthusiastic About the Great Future of His Race

Harken, O Tai Fung Po,
To the autumnal lament
Of the fallen leaves:
"What matters it to us
That the tree shall live once more
That his crooked, supplicant fingers
Shall be studded again
With buds that glimmer
Like an Emperor's precious rings?
What matters it to us
That birds shall rock upon the branches
That moon-rays, silver-hoofed,
Shall dance again to the dulcet music
Of young winds?
What matters it to us—
The dead, the fallen,
The yellow, broken leaves,
The driven wanderers of the Dusty Road?"

The Immortality That Sing Pu Longs For

Sing Pu would not regret his death
Or find it a divine injustice
If his dreams
Turned golden fireflies
Might dance
In the endless night of his brain.

Yan Yi Explains Creation

I closed slowly my eyes—
Over the still lake
A swan sailed
His breast cutting the water
Like a prow.
I opened slowly my eyes—
And the lake was still.
Thus, Lung Li,
A god closes slowly his eyes
And over the still surface
Of Time
A world sails—
He opens slowly his eyes—
And the surface of Time
Is still.

Tung Ti's Source of Melancholy

The shadows of mountains
Fall lighter than swallows' feathers
Upon the valley,
But the shadows of my memories
Fall heavy and limp
Like leaden corpses
Upon my heart.

The Ancient Poet Explains a Man's Career in Time and Space

I walked slowly through the garden
Breaking the reflection of the Moon—
The argent fragments
United again
Into a perfect circle—
But I remained in the dark.

Lo Suy Explains His Apparent Inconstancy

I am a blade of tall grass
Constant to the four white winds
Whose long finger-tips bend me
Gracefully to their whims.

Ching Hsing Advises a Poet to Avoid Meddling in the Revolution

While the storm is raging
The fragile sensitive butterfly
Hides deeply among the hospitable petals
Of the lotus flower,
His tremulous wings pasted
Tip to dazzling tip.

Yang Ho, the Scribe, Reports a Cavalcade

The Mountains are giant Camels
Plunged knee-deep
Within the scarlet sands
Of the vast Border Desert
Their fierce Riders
The Thousand Forests
Urge them
And whip them
In wild clamor
For their priceless Booty
The Sacred Ruby
The flaming Eye
Of the dying God of Day
Is falling into the Sea.

Chu-Chang Offers a Toast to His Bride, Lang Ping

Cup your small hands
Soft as the down
On the breasts of doves,
That I may press into them
Like a giant grape
My heart—
Drink,
O beloved,
The scarlet wine
Brimming with a thousand
Dreams of you!
Be drunken with me,
Always,
O Lang Ping!

Tschu-Sy Discovers That the Laws of Nature Are Capricious

Tschu-Sy's heart is heavier
Than the Grey Mountain
Whose belly is laden with ore,
But the old boat
He rows languidly
Floats upon the surface of the River
More lightly
Than a lotus petal
Newly dropped.

The Poets Sailing on the River Pa in Their Boat of Spice-Wood With the Rudder of the Precious Mulan Were Carousing and Singing the Virtues of Wine, but Han-Chun Sang "THE ODE TO MAN"

Your song, my Brother, I sing
Your woes and your hopes and your sorrows
And those unutterable silences
Which burden your spirit and your heart!

Bards have been in the meadows
And have sung of the grass and the rose
Bards have been in the woodlands
And have sung of the lark and the robin
What radiant colors are blending
To fashion the Carpet of Nature
What exquisite odors arising
Meet and mingle with the songs—
Enamored is man of the Earth.

But I shall sing of you forever!

More wondrous is your Youth than the Spring
Than Winter more noble your age
Within you are meadows and woodlands
With their budding and riping and fading
As the Morrow rises and the Night falls low
Tempestuous oceans your heart
With waves of sad lamentation
Rising and beating the shore
And asking in vain for the Truth
Changing and rushing forever
Yet eternally unaltered and still!

As sad as the wind are you
When Autumn is chilling the Earth
As gay as the butterfly sailing
When youth and sweet love are yours
Your face is the lily, the rose,
Your voice is the music of life
Your mind and your spirit
Mingle in Nirvana!

Though bards sing of mountains and forests
Though bards praise the dell and the river
Though bards sing of Earth and Sky
You alone are my theme and my song!
You with your sorrows and hopes
You with your struggles and losses
Reaching higher and higher forever
The stars your ultimate grasp
You, O my Brother, you are my song!

Sing My Lo Seeks the Ultimate

With utmost care
And impeccable precision
I tore
Petal by petal
And leaf by leaf
The lily which blossomed
In the Garden of Buddah's Temple—
Is the soul the naked stalk
Whose hard thorns
Sting me
In mockery
Or in mute revenge?

Tsing Tsi Ridicules Those Who Seek Fame by Fawning Upon the Great

Because the thick dust
The Emperor's favorite horses raised
Entered his wide nostrils
And made him sneeze
Bing Lu considers himself
An important member
Of the Imperial family.

Sung Ti-Fu Writes the Dirge of Man

Go,
Braid from the threads of Illusion
Your chain of Truth,
Weave within the vast Nightmare
Your brittle Dream,
Cull from the Froth of Time
Your Bubble Eternity,
Add to the Wail of the Winds
Your grievous sigh,
Fashion from the Dung of Death
Your Imperishable Paradise,
Sole Slave of the Earth
Sole Weeper
Sole Mourner
Lord of the Crown of Thorns
King of the hollow Scepter
Jester of the Empty Court!

Ouan Tu Writes to His Friend to Tell Him How Age Has Bowed Him

The stars which studded the Heavens
Now adorn the slimy backs of frogs
In the puddles of the road.

Tung Li Jumps From One Shore to the Other Avoiding Reality, the Bottomless Ravine

When I am sober
My thoughts are deep cups
Overbrimming with dark wine.
When I am drunk
Becoming the unwelcome guest
Of my neighbor's grunting pigs
My thoughts are crystal waters
Dancing over rocks
Refulgent
Like the virtues of Kong-Fu-Tse.

Chung Mung Si Prefers Experience to Innocence

More limpid is the Yang-Tse River
At its source
Than the silver mirror
Of a mandarin's wife,
But the fish do not dwell within it
Until it mingles
With the yellow mud
Of many hills.

Tung Tschi, the Great Lover, Explains His Melancholy

The Butterfly
Seeks Eternal Beauty
His golden wings
Are weary
With flight—

He only finds
Drops of warm honey
In the eager mouths
Of promiscuous roses.

Chu-Ping the Conqueror Gazes at the Horizon and Hears "The Voice of the Earth"—He Quits His Palace and Becomes an Itinerant Beggar

Who calls himself master
Who names himself owner
Who dares enyoke me
To serve him alone?
Knows he the ages
That ploughed me and died?
Sees he the footprints
Left on my heart?
Nations are sleeping
Tier upon tier
Worlds in their slumber
Melted in me!

Fierce was the struggle
Gigantic the effort
One seed to create
Deep tore man's nails
To open my womb
Long were the ages
'Twixt the germ and the grain!

Not pure was the lily
Not fragrant the rose
Not tall grew the cedar

Not soft lay the grass
Till man in his agony
Fed each with his blood!

Thinks he yon pebble
Is stone but or mortar?
Within it are buried
The travails of ages.

Entombed in my mountains
And crushed lies humanity
That dug in the darkness
For iron and gold
Trackless the ocean
Rolls on forever
While hiding beneath her
The measureless tomb
And her groans inarticulate
Reecho the anguish
Of a mankind that drowning
Conquered the wave.

The sands of the desert
Are smoothed by the winds
No longer recalled now
Is the form of the buried
For onward continued
The wearisome caravans
Till beneath them
Lo! sprouted
The garden and the field!

Rough and inclement
Were the paths that were trod
Slow and unyielding
Were the walls of the Night

Mighty were Falsehood
And the Giant Fear
Bitter the warfare
From ape unto man!

Erased are the steps now
Forgotten the shoulders
Which uplifted the feet
Nameless the spirits
That invented and thought.

But deep in my bosom
I carry the record
Each hand that has touched me
Each foot that has crossed me
Each nation that added
One blade to my grass
'Tis thus I can answer
In roses and lilies
'Tis thus I can carry
The forests and fields
'Tis thus I am mother
And feed all the world.

Who dares be my master
Who names himself King?
What jewels can purchase
One atom of me?
Each step on my bosom
Is a step on all nations
Each grain that is sprouting
Draws life from all ages.

What hand dare enfence me
And say: "THIS IS MINE!"

To Jen Hsin, Who Complains That Nowadays One Cannot Keep His Soul Intact

On the crests of turbulent waves
Petals of roses ride.

Tsu Po Answers Condemnation for Subjectivity in His Art

Does not the timorous sparrow
Bend over the fountain rim
And drink the water
Out of the fluttering shadow
Of its own beak?

Fung Ku Tchi Outwits Nemesis

When I was happy
And had love, abundant
Like the grasses in Summer
I sang of the sorrow of Life
And beauty's evanescent glory
Fearing the jealousy of the Silent God
That is more bitter than the weeds
Witches cull on moonless nights.
Now that I am wretched
And my solitude wearies me
Like a shoreless desert
I sing of the Joy of Living
And Beauty's imperishable luster
Fearing the rancor of the Silent God
Which pierces more sharply
Than a serpent's cloven tongue.

Ping Chi Yearns to Be in the Perfect Harmony of the Universe

Ping Chi, Composer of immortal music,
Drinks from the golden goblet
Which graces the Imperial table
Until his laurelled head
Turns and spins
In a dolorous futile circle.

To Cho Tu, Who Hopes to Be Remembered by Mankind Because of His Many Fine Deeds

Does the river
Remember
O To Cho Tu,
The many clouds
Which made its waters
Or the rock
The multitudinous shapes
Of its grains of sand?

Fung Tchu Si Bemoans the Ingratitude of Things

For the hundred generations
Of green and red leaves
That danced upon him
The mad cotillions of Wind and Rain
The giant Oak has a hundred scars
That strangle him
Like iron hoops
And a great hollowness.

Ki Kang Watches Time

In the morning
The rose
At my window
Was a voluptuous lady
Awaiting the kiss of her lover—
In the evening
Petals shrunken
Perfume scattered
She was an ancient harlot
Shaking dolefully—
Time,
The Worm,
Is crawling
Over the stem. . .

Fan Ch'i Seeks the Ultimate Truth

The famished alley cat
Captured the dazzling bird
Song still throbbing
In its tender throat—
God of All Things
You who were both the hungry cat
And the rapturous bird
And who are now only the purring feline
Licking its chops
Scattered bloody feathers
And the vague echo of a song
Riding on the dying wind,
Have you been appeased?

Do you live in serene contentment
Within the stuffed maw?
O Great Creator
Father of Stars and Suns
Lord of All Wisdom,
Is this your Ultimate Truth
This the Cosmic Decree
Eternal and immutable:
"Eat one Another
For I am the Devourer
And the Devoured!"

Tsang Wu-Chung's Parable of Disillusion

I

The Iceberg
Glides on
Slowly
Ponderously
Remembering
In vast bitterness
That a myriad years ago
He believed the Sun
Was the Great White Flame
Which would melt him
Into a Sea
Measureless
Roaring
Lashing
The ribs of all the shores
Juggling
Upon his foamy finger tips
Giant whales

And colossal boats
And drowning
In playful mischief
The supercilious Moon—
Now
The Iceberg knows
The Sun is but the shadow
Cold
Glaring
Of himself
Pursuing him
As he glides on
Forever
In frigid massiveness
Seagulls riding
Triumphantly
Upon his crest.

II

The Sun
Spins on
Dizzily
Inexorably
Remembering
In vast bitterness
That a myriad years ago
He believed the Iceberg
Was the Great White Anvil
Against which his rays
Mighty hammers
Would strike
A million million Stars
Dancing athwart
The countless galaxies
Turning them into black ashes
Plunging into the yawning mouth
Of Infinite Chaos—

Now
The Sun knows
The Iceberg is but the shadow
Flabby
Glassy
Of himself
Pursuing him
As he spins on
Forever
In the immense Hollowness
Weaving
Gold and silver carpets
Into shivering puddles
For ducks and geese
To sail upon
In regal pomp.

Yu Chung Expounds the Idea of Equality

I crushed a flower
A perfect flower
In playfulness
And cast it away

I broke a heart
A perfect heart
In playfulness
And cast it away

I crushed a flower
I broke a heart.

Mah Ah Fu, Mendicant Friar, Appeals to the Young Poets of Cathay

Sing the Song of Today
Sing the Song of this Hour
Burdened with breathing humanity
Its rage and its hopes and its sorrows
The vast tumultuous cataract of Life.
The others have sung of the past
Of the prowess of kings and of princes
Giants who trampled on cities
And flooded the nations with blood.
Sing the Song of Today
The song of the men and the women
Who conquer the Earth by their toil
And bring surcease to the ill and the worn
The Song of the living Sages
Who hurl their shafts at lies and wrongs
Proclaiming Justice and Truth!
Sing of the lowly young who battle and fail
Of the inglorious old who languish forsaken
Sing the Song of Today
The Song of the Hour that lives!

Chang-Kan-Ton, Forsaken Mistress, Bemoans Her Fate

"My love is a red red rose!"
Ah me, had I but guessed the meaning of your words!
A rose indeed was the love you bore me
It blossomed and blazed one day
And spread its delicate scent,

But night came
Dark and icy
And petal by petal dropped
And the wind swept them
And mingled them
With the mud and the dust of the road
Leaving me only the naked thorny stalk
Of bitter emptiness.
A rose was the love you bore me
Would it had been rock and earth
Homely and rugged and hard
But defying the ice of night
And the howling of wind!
Ah me, had I but guessed the meaning of your words!

Kung-Ye Chan'g, Writer of Comedies, Explains His Creations

You complain,
Wa Mi, ancient Friend,
Who slept with me under one cover at night,
That my work is frivolous
And therefore transitory
As the clouds that winds drive
Across fields and ponds
With their pouting mouths
And you advise me to create
Works grave and solemn
As the stately Green Mountain
We used to gaze at
From my humble threshold
And which the angry fangs of Time
Gnaw in vain.

Watch,
O Wa Mi,
Some night of Spring
The frivolous rays
Of the Full Moon
Pirouette merrily
Upon the noses of the leaves
While the weariest breeze
Opening its mouth
In a casual yawn
Crumbles them
Into glittering fragments—
Yet far beyond the Green Mountain
Tragic
Immutable
The imperishable White Skull
Sets ablaze the Deserts
And churns the rimless Seas—
My works, too,
O ancient Friend,
Are refulgent rays
Pirouetting irreverently
Upon the noses of men
A languid finger flips them
And laughter scatters them
In gleeful disarray—
Yet far beyond the Horizon
The White Skull of Truth
Whence they flow
Tragic
Immutable
Sets ablaze minds
And churns unbounded spirits.

Ki K'ang Asks a Question and Receives an Answer

O Kung-Fu-Tse,
Master of the Good Conduct
Father of the Perfect Decorum,
Considering the behavior of the World
Her wrongs
Her lies
Her follies,
What is the proper way
Of greeting her—
Face in the dust
Or erect?
Obedient
Or defiant?
Hailing
Or haranguing?
Weeping
Or laughing?

Ki K'ang, dutiful Son,
The World is but a mirror
And all our gestures
Are made before the shadow
We cast upon it.

Fung Li, Fisherman, Consoles Himself

Fung Li throws his net
For gold and silver fish—
Fung Li's net is heavy
With weeds and broken shells—
"The Sea is barren,
For the Moon, her Lover,
Is old."

Woe to the Great Who Outlive Their Fame

The old mastiff
Conqueror of wolves and foxes
Lies huddled in a corner
Pestered by flies
And spat upon
By small kittens.

Mi Tsi Advises a Poet Not to Despair

At the right moment
The Earth smiles—
Between her lips
Slightly parted
A daisy trembles
In sheer delight.

Yen Yu Would Drive a Bargain With Time

You will strip me bare
O Time
Of all that Illusion
Has called my own—
Youth
And Love
And Hopes
And Immortal Projects
You will turn
Diamond into glass

Gold into straw
Robe into rag
Fortune into dust.
I cannot stay your Hand
Nor will I pray respite,
Yet this alone I beg
That till my bark
Drop into the Bottomless Gulf
You do not choke
The crystalline stream
That gurgles through
My Mountain of Debris:
LAUGHTER.

Yen Chow-Yew Is Reconciled to the Inevitable

Winter has caught
The little Stream
By her silver feet
That clattered against the rocks
As clatter the spurs
Of a merry cavalier.
She tugs
And pulls
But her heavy sides
Like frozen tongues
Lick in impotence
The glassy stones.
Soon,
Wiser with the anguish
She will lie still
And like some colossal dead eye
Will mirror the dreams
Of clouds and winds.

Wung Li Preaches the Importance of Non-Importance

The wind bends and breaks
The proud branch
Of the tall tree
And scatters its leaves
In the dust of the road,
But the shadow of the pebble
Remains stiff and immovable
A black iron nail
Deeply driven into the Earth.

Fan Ch'i Yearns for His Sweetheart's First Song

Once
Upon a summer night
We were alone
And she, wisely artless,
Intoned a melody
So simple
And so wondrous strange
My heart opened
And all the Universe
Flowed in
And overbrimmed it.
So often since
Have Autumns chased
The stiffened leaves
Across the frozen road
And sepulchral moons glared
Among the desolate branches,
So often since
We were alone
And she sang

A hundred subtle melodies
But nevermore
Could she intone
The one upon that summer night
So simple
And so wondrous strange
And nevermore
My heart opened
And all the Universe
Flowed in
And overbrimmed it.

The Mirror Reminisces and the Fate of Su Shu Huang, Poet Laureate

Night after night
The two sat together
On the sofa
And laughed—
Then she sat alone
And wept.

Every morning
She stared at me
And viciously
Plucked white threads
From her head.

The fat clumsy woman
Who for days
Scorned to gaze at me
Was the pretty bride
Who danced
Before me
For hours.

In an angle
Of me
There was a box
Long and black—
People passed
Bent over it
And wept.

Day after day
The boy pushed
His face
Into me
Trying to go beyond
And he puffed
And puffed
His cheeks
But he only flattened
And reddened his nose
And hurt his jaws.

Did he not know
That I am the Terminus
The Ultimate Horizon
The World's Immovable Barrier?
Does not everybody know
That I am the Net
That captures all things?
That I open my eye
And all things are
That I close my eye
And all things vanish?
That without me
There are only shadows
Crawling backward?
That I transmute them
Into realities

Flowing forward?
Does not everybody know
That all is silence
Forever,
And that they who puff
To utter sounds
Do but contort
Grotesquely?

Once
A man
Gazed at me
For a long while
Motionless
As if seeking something
That had fallen
Into me
Long ago.
Suddenly
He pressed a gun
Into his temple—
A stream
Black and red
Gushed out of him
And he fell
His face against the floor
And never stirred.
A moth
Flew about him
In circles—
Then
Wings pasted
Tip to tip
Alighted
Upon his head.

Wan Chang Rejects the Lie of Love

Roses succumb with the day
Fields with the seasons die
Rocks from the mountains sever
Blood and spirit turn to clay
How then should our love bloom on forever?
Tombs are the roots of things
Dirges we tap with our feet
Death is the Master Supernal
Unchallenged the final defeat
Why do we lie that our love is eternal?

Wu-shuh Is in a Quandary

The great mountains are black clouds
Moving across the sky
Slowly
Like weary elephants
Heavily laden—
The black clouds opposite
Are great mountains
Solid and impenetrable
Like giant bears
Nailed to the Sky—
O wise Master K'Ung of Lu,
How shall weak-eyed and deluded Man
Distinguish the True from the False?

Ku Hung Dissuades His Friend, Po Yi, From Becoming a Monk

To gain Heaven, Po Yi, is very simple—
Place a bowl of clear water
Upon your threshold
Some moonlit night
And Heaven, on tip-toes
Softer than the foot-fall
Of a wary wolf at dawn
Shall come
Timorously at your door.
But how shall we gain Earth
Mad, whimsical Earth,
The laughing Dancer
Dancing upon the far-flung tips
Of the Sun?
Oh, how shall we gain Earth,
Po Yi, my ancient friend?

Yang Ho Bemoans the Way of Things

You no longer think of me
Nor I of you
The love we bore each other
Has vanished as the shadow
Of the chirping sparrow
Hopping on the grasses
Leaving neither sign nor scar.
Our hearts emptied of their song
Beat against our chests
Like sticks upon dreary drums

And yet we had vowed
By the sacred and eternal ashes
Of our noble ancestors
That neither Time nor Hazard
Would sever us—
Alas, ashes are deaf
And remember nothing
Time is a hammer
Smashing vows
And Hazard is Master of All.

Kieh-Nih Is Grateful for the Hospitality

Autumn
Most gracious Host
Ordered his slaves
The cunning old Winds
To soften my path
With thick carpets and rugs
Of yellow and red leaves
And dainty petals of flowers
And blow through half-closed fists
The merry music
Of regal welcome,
While the black Trees
Naked old Negroes
Captured young wingless Winds
And beat their rough arms
Against their white bellies
The March of the Flying Birds. . . .
Dazzled by the honor
I bowed most humbly
And bent
And shivering
I hastened my step.

Ma Fu Wung Ridicules the Pretentious

THE SQUIRREL:

I grip the World
In my great upper paws
I crack it with my mighty teeth
I fill my vast cheeks
With its savory kernel
And devour it—
I am the Lord of the Universe!

THE CLOUD:

I extinguish the Sun
And blind the Moon
And all the stars.
I proclaim to the Cosmos:
"Let there be Darkness!"
I am the God of the Night!

THE GOOSE:

I am the Goddess of Bounty
With divine largesse
I lay for Man
The glowing fruit
Of my fertile womb.
If ever I die
Alas for him!
He will perish
In the toils of hunger
And the dust of penury.

THE LOG:

I am the Master of the River
I float upon it
In majestic elegance
I hold the water
Within its shores
And lead it
Securely
From the lofty mountain
To the salty sea.

THE WEATHERCOCK:

I am King of the Winds
I order their courses:
"To the East!
To the West!
Blow!
Blow!"
I draw the reins
About their white necks:
"To the North!
To the South!
Blow!
Blow!"
I drop the reins
And command:
"Stop!
Stop!"
And all the Winds
Those of the North
And those of the South
Those of the East
And those of the West
Drop at my feet
And sleep.

Chu Ming, Practical Poet, Gains Heaven and Earth

At night
Chu Ming hurls his net against the sky
And captures stars
Which he squanders with regal prodigality
Among his dear and learned friends
As they empty many cups of wine.
At day
Chu Ming casts his net into the river
And captures fish
Which he offers with fastidious prudence
To the thrifty wives of the Imperial City
Haggling minutely over prices.

Ki Fu Speaks of the Difference Between Merit and Position

Riding majestically
The horse borrowed of his neighbor
Wing Lu, the Pigmy,
Considers himself the tallest man
Within the ancient and impregnable walls
Of the Eternal Empire.

Pang Chu Shen Presents the Magic Circus of His Love

1.

My Love
Merry clown
Throws kisses
Red Balloons
Which crack
Upon my lips
In joyous thunderclaps.

2.

Her eyes
Dazzling Suns
Dance
On silver toes
I flap my wings
And crow
Triumphant:
"It is morning!"

3.

I
Weary Camel
Dreaming
She
Fluffy Sparrow
Perching
Suddenly
Upon the peak
Of my hump.

4.

My Melancholy
Gloomy Bear
Tearing at his chain
My Love
Fearless Tamer
Whips him
And makes him dance
Daintily.

5.

My Patience
Ponderous Elephant
Flaps his great ears
Blinking
Her whims
Cunning Monkeys
Play hide-and-seek
Between his legs.

6.

Her Laughter
Bareback Rider
Cracks the hoops
Of dull hours
In long rows
And turns sommersaults
On the grey back
Of my Soul.

7.

Her Breasts
Two tender Lambs
Hide
Shivering
In mock terror

From the famished
Untamed Wolves
My Fingers.

8.

Her hair
Black Fox
Sleeping
Beneath
The setting sun
My Eyes
Wary hunters
Watching.

9.

Her Singing
Gentle murmur
Over milky
Rocks
My thoughts
Restless Tigers
Licking their paws
Purring.

10.

My Love
And I
A magic Circus
Red Balloons
Cracking
Upon the Lips
Of Time
In joyous thunderclaps.

Amah Ah Fu Weighs the World

The World is light—
I carry it all
Sun and Moon
The great Mountains
And the tumultuous Seas
In the pupils of my eyes—
For fear of spilling it
I walk slowly
Carefully
With balanced steps,
While Death,
The Shadow of Myself,
Runs now before me
Now behind
Like a faithful mastiff.

Sing Pu Answers His Friend Who Asked Him How to Acquire Perfect Happiness

What is the bait,
O Kung Chang,
That will tempt
The Moon swimming in your fountain?

Kung Han Finds Trifles More Dangerous Than Great Events

Because of a few sparks
The town of Shang-Hi turned to ashes,
But the vast flames of the setting Sun
Rain in vain upon the dry haystack
That stands in Mi Tzu's farm.

Ti Fu Rebukes a Vain Man

The branches laden with fruit
Bend humbly to the ground.

Ling To Speaks of the Impossibility of Altering One's Fate

At midnight
Sing Chi, Astrologer of the Son of Heaven,
Hurled angrily into the White River
Many sharp-pointed stones
Exclaiming:
"Crumble, my evil star!"

Chung-Ne's Dilemma

How shall I walk upon you,
O Earth,
How shall I crush beneath my feet
Ten thousand generations of men?
Forgive me,
O Master Kong-Fu-Tse,
Whose virtue is full
And doctrine complete,
If grains of you
Mingled with the manure
My bare feet stepped into
As I walked to the Temple
To do homage to your Name.

Shuh-Sun's Prayer to His Beloved

Your love,
Yang Kuei-Fei,
Is a chain
At which I tug and pull
Seeking escape—
Make it stronger
I pray you
Lest I break it.

Tsz-Chang, Eminent Theologian, Explains the Way of Death and Immortality

Yesterday
I was a flame
That dipped and rose
Like a giant red bird
In flight over the Sea.
Today
I am a heap of ashes
Cold and grey
Like a bone
Dried of marrow
Which dogs disdain—
O good Wind
Carry me gently
In your white arms
And lower me
Into the Marvellous Pond
Of the Marvellous Park
Where ashes burst
Into flames
Unquenchable
Eternal.

Hwuy Of Leang Warns His Son of the Wiles and Dangers of Love

Should the red-mouthed Flame
Warn the dizzy enamored Moth:
"Do not approach me,
O Fool,

Fly through the thin crevice
Of the closed window
For my breath is cruel and mighty
And turns gaudy-colored wings
Into scattered specks
Of brown ashes!"
And if the Moth be deaf
And obstinate
Should the Flame whistle out its soul
Shut its great scarlet eye
And vanish
Remorseful
A shapeless thread
On the shoulder
Of a passing Wind?

Kih Tsz-Shing, Imperial Horticulturist, Records Dialogues Between Leaves and Wind

It was summer
And the leaves on the trees
Nodded and swayed
To the piping of the young wind.

LEAVES:

Pray, O Master Wind,
Let us sail
Upon your soft white breast
As the birds and the butterflies sail!

Break the fetters
That enchain us
To the whipping sticks
And the old gnarled logs
Whose feet are buried
In the filthy mud
Crawling with worms and ants!
O good Wind
Carry us far far away
To that dazzling Land
Where silver stars squat
Upon the golden carpets of the Sun
And wingèd Leaves
Dance to the music of the Moon!
O gentle Wind
Let us sail
Upon your soft white breast!

WIND:

In the ripeness of Time
Your wish shall be granted
And your fetters shall be shattered—
In the ripeness of Time.

It was Autumn
And the leaves on the trees
Rattled and shivered
To the howling of the old wind.

LEAVES:

Pray, O Master Wind,
Give us peace!
Your mouth scorches us
And your claws tear us asunder—
O Mighty Wind,

Go far far away
Over the Great Waters
Across the Tall Mountains
And leave us alone!

WIND:

It is the ripeness of Time—
I have come to shatter your fetters
And free you from the whipping sticks
And the old logs
As you have bidden me.

LEAVES:

Why have you changed,
O Master Wind,
Why is your mouth fire
And your breast ice?

WIND:

It is the ripeness of Time.

LEAVES:

What shall become of us,
O wicked Wind,
O cruel Wind?

WIND:

You shall be the manure
To the new leaves.

Tso-K'iou Foretells His Destiny

I am a Clown
Plastered face
Scarlet mouth
Tawny wig—
I juggle upon my false nose
The Great Ass's Bladder
The Earth and her myriad Moons—
The people crack sunflower seeds
And laugh.

In a thousand reincarnations
I shall be a Buddha—
Vast belly
Enormous jowls
Six pairs of arms
Blazing with gems—
I shall juggle upon my false hands
The Great Bull's Horn
The Heavens and her myriad Gods—
The people shall light torches
And bow before me
Their noses in the dust.

Tsai Wo, the Rebel, Condemned to be Beheaded, Warns His Judges the Old Must Die!

As when the Wind shakes the tree
Calling out:
"Make room for the New!"
The withered and shriveled leaves
Rattle and groan

And hug the broken twigs
And the cleaved branches,
But in vain
They are swept into the gutter—
So when Time shakes the walls
Of the ancient town
Calling out:
"Make room for the Young!"
Wild is the clamor
Of those withered with hate
And those shriveled with folly
Hugging the rotting pillars
Of hoary and hallowed crimes
And hiding beneath the ermine
And the stately arrogance
Guilt strangling Innocence
And Falsehood shackling Truth,
But in vain
The Wind of Youth shall sweep them
Their evil name blotted
Their foul fabrics buried—
THE OLD MUST DIE!

Chen Ching-Hsuan Has a Change of Heart

I was sullen and dejected
And hurled maledictions
At Man the fool
And Woman the fiend
Earth the charnel house
And Gods the myriad-mouthed Worms
Devourers of All,
When suddenly
I turned my gaze
Upon the garden
Which only yesternight
Was a desert of dusty limbs
But now glowed with a thousand buds
Each washed with the cool
Waters of the dew.
And lo, my heart leaped
As leaps a gracious dancer
In joyous flutter
And I scattered blessings
At Man the wise
And Woman the good
Earth the bounteous Womb
And Gods the myriad-winged Bees,
Carriers of Life.

Ling Mo Discourses on the Meaning of Values

The great poet fell into the river
And drowned,
But the feather the sparrow dropped
Floated like a tiny boat
Over the wide circles
That wrinkled the water.

Bing Si Advises a Lady Not to Despair Because of the Malignity of People's Tongues

Should the luminous Moon
Dash despondent
Against a passing Star
Because the dogs
Squatting at the doors
Of their miserable kennels
Bark at her
Their jaws pasting
With yellow foam?

Tsang Wu-Chang Faces Reality

Death stands in the corner
And grins—
I turn my back upon him
And live—
Clownish things provoke my throat
I bend upon myself
And laugh—
Sorrows gather in my eyes
I hide my face
And weep—
And Morning
And Night
False sentinels
Let the years,
The subtle Thieves,

Pass them
Their arms laden with my treasures
And vanish—
In dread
In stealth
I turn
And look—
Death stands in the corner
And grins.

Tsi Fu Finds Ambition Tantamount to Vulgarity and Greed

Seeing that the bountiful
And the most impartial gods
Rewarded all
Indiscriminately
With the glory of Death,
Tsi Fu considered the ambitious
Vulgar and greedy
Saying:
"Does not one laurel suffice
For one head?"

Wing Tsi Is Inclined to Consider Death a Pleasant Experience

When I stretch out upon my bed
I utter a deep sigh of relief
As if I found a dear friend
Long considered lost.

When the cock crows
And I must rise
I yawn loudly many times
Grumbling against the intrusion
Of the heavy-footed Sun,
Crusher of dreams.

Mang Kung-Ch'oh Bids Farewell to His False Love

Last night you lay within my arms
Your kisses deep and long
As subtle flames consumed me
And all the Universe vanished. . .
Today I lay alone
My mind wandering
Within a forest of thoughts
When suddenly you appeared
As a blazing Sun appears
Breaking through heavy clouds—
I held you in my arms
And your kisses deep and long
As subtle flames consumed me
And all the Universe vanished. . .
You have left me
And as days follow days
Whom will my mind recall—
You or the dream of you?

Loh Shang-Teh Believes that Free Will Is an Illusion

DESTINY:

I am loosening
The iron bar
Hanging across
The roof of this house.
It shall balance
In the air
As if held
By a thread.
I am speeding
The gait
Of this man
Who is going home
To tell his wife
Of his unexpected
Good fortune.
I am leading
His steps
Precisely underneath
The swinging bar
And I am blowing
A wind across it.
In this fraction
Of time
When Reality
Emerges from the womb
Of Non-Existence
The iron bar
Strikes the man's head
With a thunderous clap.

The man wriggles
And the road is splashed
With black
And red blood. . .
Thus
It has come to pass
As it was ordained
By the billion links
In the chain of Eternity
That at this instant
This bit of space
In the Universe
Has become wet
Without the need of rain.

Tsin T'ang Explains Why He Has Written a Cynical Poem

Finding life the clamorous love-making
Of mangy cats
In the backyard of Time
I barked.

Fung Si Speaks of the Uselessness of Taking Too Much Care of Oneself

The flower
However nurtured
Must wither
Crushed
Between the stony fingers
Of the inevitable Autumn.

Fung Chi Tells His Friend Not to Be Angry Against Those Who Having Succeeded Forget Their Humble Origin

Should the Butterfly
Knight of the blossoming Rose
Remember the slimy worm
Crawler of barks of trees?

Li Po Laments the Frailty of Old Age Even When Apparently Vigorous

In Spring the leaves are firm
Upon the branches of the trees
Though the winds be sharp
Like the long-pointed teeth
Of famished wolves.
In Autumn the leaves shiver and drop
Though the winds be faint
Like the fragile steps of mice
Fleeing from one safety place to another
Through a crowded room.

Si Tchung Tells Why He Has Abandoned His Unprofitable Career as Artist and Taken to Fishing

The praises of the world
Were shadows of rainbows
With which I tried in vain
To fill my basket.

The fish of the Great Lake,
O beloved friend,
Overbrim it
Sleeping
Peacefully
Their mouths wide open
Like lusty choristers.

Chang Ku Claims That Even the Apparent Impersonal Philosophy Is but a Species of Consolation

Being very short
Wang Gu Chin
Famous philosopher
Wrote a long treatise
Criticizing bitterly
Those too-far-removed
From the good Earth
Mother Immortal
Perfect Teacher
Of the Perfect Truth.

T'ang Ti Bewails His Circumstances

I am a kite swollen with wind
Yearning to fly to the stars
Alas, my feet are heavy ropes
Holding me just above the roofs.

Tsing Kung Tells His Friend to Beware of Docile People Becoming Angry

In winter the trees are porcupines
Whose short stiff quills tear
The ashen face of the Wind.

The Compassion of Sung Ti-Fu, Theologian

I pity you,
God of the Universe,
I pity the unassuaged loneliness
And the unendurable boredom
That impelled you to create—
I pity the magical hands
Which endeavored to fashion
Out of shapeless Void
Life and Happiness,
But through artless ignorance
Or in grievous error
Molded Sorrow and Death.
Now the Universe rejects you
No Star, no Moon in infinite Space
Offers you asylum,
And Man, astray and forsaken
In the wilderness of Vastness
His Earth a desolate speck
Whirling in blind confusion
Within the night of clouds
Supplicates your blessings
In monotonous futility,
While you, blind and deaf,

Squat at the uttermost rim
Where eternal Chaos reigns
Your paralyzed hands
Fallen upon your lap
Moaning hopelessly
Without end:
"To die! To die! To die!"

T'ai-Pih Celebrates an Anniversary

Ten years ago upon this day
I came to you as comes a stranger
Equipped with lies and flattery
And an empty heart
Yet I know not how
Before an hour passed
I sat perplexed and piqued
"Mistress Hai-Shish is playing the ancient game,
It is well.
I know all the tricks.
I am fully armored."
And I laughed.
But soon the game became a mortal combat
I parried blow for blow
I struggled and floundered
And battered and disarmed
I pleaded:
"I surrender, O Hai-Shish!"

And the years have passed
Spring and Winter
Have mocked each other
In their futile chase

Old moons have died
New moons were born
And still I sit and wonder
How ten years ago upon this day
I came to you as a stranger
Equipped with lies and flattery
And an empty heart
And fought a battle
Fierce and relentless
But lost in utter disarray
And became your slave
And I still am,
O Hai-Shish!

Kang Cheng Considers the Meaning of Freedom

The rebellious wave
Curved
Like the threatening beak
Of a giant eagle
Tore the reins
That harnessed it
To the galloping tide
Of the White Sea
Splashed triumphantly
The rocky shore—
And mingled with the sands.

Mi Lung Complains Against Time

Why does the mad Stallion
Dashing
His great body
Bathed in foam
Crush under his iron hoofs
The dainty flowers
Of my small garden?

The Sermon on Perfection by Yu Po, Venerable Philosopher, Delivered at the Gate of Heavenly Peace Before His Departure

Be humble!
Consider your life, O Man,
The pain of its birth
The pang of its death
The sorrows and the torments
Of its numbered years!
Be humble!
How are you greater
Than the bird you shoot
Than the bee you rob
Than the pig you roast?
Be humble!
Do you know why the wind moans
Among the leaves?
Why the night lies thoughtful
Over the day?
Why the waves unconsoled
Forever hurl themselves
Against the rocks?

Be humble!
What flame in your lighthouse
Is brighter than the torch
In the tail of the firefly?
What vision in your sage's mind
Is as lustrous as the silk
The worm spins around itself?
What plan in your builder's chart
Is as subtle as the bridge
The spider stretches twixt the branches
And the dawn fills with gems?
Be humble!
What empress has a skin
As soft as the petal of the lotus?
A breath as sweet
As that of the rose?
A voice as dulcet
As that of the nightingale?
Be humble!
Have you the sight of the eagle
The strength of the elephant
The fleetness of the deer
The patience of the ant?
Be humble!
Consider, O Man,
Your malice
Your rancor
Your wars
Your iniquities!
Be humble!
Remember that the great is small
And the small great
That the palace is a hut
And the hut a palace

That good is evil
And evil good
That truth is lie
And lie truth
That dream is deed
And deed dream
That body is shadow
And shadow body
That love is hate
And hate love
That folly is wisdom
And wisdom folly
That Life and Death
Have equal weight
On the Balance of Time.
Be humble!

Chang Hsu Warns All Tyrants

Ice
Merciless Tyrant
Lies heavily
Upon the River,
But deep underneath
There is the mighty roaring
Of the rebel Spirit
Of the Waters—
And Spring comes
And woe to the Tyrant!

Wing Mu Si Speaks of the Vanity of Man's Illusions

The souls of men
Are birds with beaks of glass
Which break
Knocking
At the adamantine gates
Of Paradise.

Lung Li Writes a Friend's Biography

Your life was a desert, prostrate
Dreaming of rain.
Your death was a long shivering
In a grey tempest.
Your coffin was a giant sensitive plant
Capturing a yellow fly.
Your funeral was a thought of Night
Lost on the dazzling shores of Day
Running to hide itself.
Your eternity is a tall stone
The years, dusty Masons,
Are hammering on. . .
Rest in peace!

Ha Han Si Finds the Search of Absolute Perfection Disastrous

T'ang Wu, the sculptor,
Chiselled at his masterpiece
Until it lay upon the floor
A shapeless mass
Of stone and white dust.

Han Hu Believes that Pleasure Is but Relief From Pain

Having read about the long preparations
For the festivities at the Imperial Court,
Han Hu shook his head sadly,
And asked:
"Is their suffering so great, in truth,
Needing such pleasures to forget?"

Gan Ha, Exquisite Lyrist, Appreciated by the Learned, Would Prefer to Become a Popular Story-Teller

The nightingale whose golden notes
Delight the Imperial Court
Yearns to be a pompous rooster
Crowing on the peak of a dung-hill
That all the neighbors might hear him
And say:
"Let us awaken! It is morning!"

Ki K'ang, Buddhist Priest, Ill, Sings Praises to Death

O Death
You have granted man love
You have taught man mercy
You have borne man peace.
O Death
What were existence
Unceasing forever?
Wounds never healed
Travail unending.
O Death
Freer is your tomb
Than the prison of Life
Sweeter your stillness
Than the storm of passion.
O Death
Teacher of wisdom
Gauger of Values
Harbinger of Truth.
O Death
River of Silence
Quencher of Flame
Assuager of Anguish.
O Death
Lay your hand
Upon my eyelids
Tighten your fingers
About my nostrils
Press your fist
Against my heart.
O Death
O Great Gate
To Eternal Nirvana
Open!
Let me enter!

Yen Hwui, Teacher of Princes, Cautions His Pupils About the Vagaries of Glory and Power by the Parable of the Quarry

QUARRY:

From my vast bowels
Men gathered marble
Dazzling and flaming
Like the moons of the desert
And built temples
Whose beauty daunted and awed
And filled them with gods
Who towered over the Earth
Scattering sorrow and death
As peasants scatter
Seeds into plowed land
And magnificent palaces
Wherein ruled kings and emperors
Whose emblazoned splendor
Bowed princes into submission.

All has vanished
Temples and gods
And kings and emperors
Swept into the rivers
My ripped bowels
Sealed with iron dust
My name and place forgotten—
All—all—vanished
Save the jagged chips
Clotted with blood
And buried in the mud
With which the howling mob
Slayed the Perfect Sage
Who taught Master K'ung of Lu
The Good Way and the Golden Rule.

Ku T'ang Si Asks for an Epitaph

Since nothing exists save words,
When I am dead,
O citizens of the Lower Valley,
Carve upon my tombstone:
"One who suffers from Forgetfulness."

To Li Lo, Metaphysician

The hoop rolled about itself
Seeking the ultimate point
Of its subtle tail.

Tung Ching Complains Against His Beloved Who Never Reciprocated His Affections

A butterfly
Perched
Upon the shadow
Of a rose
Seeking honey.

Po Li, Astronomer, Discovers a Discrepancy in the Universe

Has Nature changed her way
That Noon comes dancing
In the midst of Night?
It is the luminous face
Of my beloved
Flooding the room!

Tsang Sin Complains Against His Dreams

Why do you vanish
O my Dreams
Like wild birds
At the tread of the hunter
The moment I try to mold you?

Why do your wondrous melodies
Turn to dying echoes
When I seek to lock them
Forever treasured
In my heart?

You build a magical temple
But the instant I place my foot
Upon the threshold
To worship within
It crumbles into dust.

You spread before me
A garden of rarest flowers

I bend to pluck
One single bud
Lo, it is a desert.

You pour a cataract
Of dazzling jewels
I reach to cull them
I find but a spider's web
Heavy with dead flies.

From the flame of a star
You weave me eternal love
I rush to enfold her
I gather a fistful of ashes
And searing embers of regret.

You taunt me
You mock me
You delude me,
But forsake me never
O my Dreams!

Po Li Tschi Writes to His Sweetheart, Who Is Far Away, How He Will Make Her Return at Once

I shall squeeze Space
Until the Earth is not wider
Than a footstep
And shall crumble Time
Until the year
Expires
In one heart beat.

Po Lo, Mistrusting His Sweetheart Who Generally Finds a New Love Before the Old One Is Dead, Asks a Question in Geology

The heart of my Beloved
Is a heaven with two suns—
One plunges its molten silver
In a dazzling cataract—
The other dies
In anguish
In a shallow pool of blood.
Tell me,
O Beloved,
How long before a cataract
Shrinks into a shallow pool?

Su Yin-Tsang Does Not Believe That Hard Labor Necessarily Produces Works of Art

The Ocean was in labor—
Shc tossed in great agony
On her measureless bed.
Her tumultuous cries
Terrified sailors and fishermen
And their wives at all the shores
Wept and prayed to all the Buddhas.
But wondrous would be the things
The Ocean's vast womb would deliver:
Scarlet lands of glowing corals,
Sunken cargoes of gold and diamonds,
Seaports drowned millennia ago,

Moons that loved her and died
And dropped into her limitless caverns,
A young Ocean that would crack the Earth
And whose waves would drown the skies. . .

The Ocean was still
Save for the gentle rocking
By the sleepy Moon,
And her murmur was sweet and comforting
To sailors and fishermen,
And their wives at all the shores
Laughed and praised all the Buddhas. . .
On the yellow and white sands
Lay the offsprings of the travail:
Empty shells
Slimy weeds
Dead gulls. . .

Han Su, Having Found at Last the Middle Course, Dies

In youth, the sun burnt Han Su too strongly,
In middle age, the shadows made him shiver,
When he became old, he learned at last
To sit underneath trees
Whose leaves made patterns
Of light and shade
Breaking in precise proportions
The rays of the sun—
But Night set in suddenly.

Tsing Lu Speaks of the Futility of Ambition

Every time Fung Mi
Was called the greatest conqueror
Of his generation
He answered sadly:
"Is not Death always
The greatest conqueror
Of each generation?"

Chan Kung Yee's Will and Testament

I bequethe
All I own—
My dreams
My thoughts
My hopes
My loves
To my constant Companion
To him who was faithful
In a faithless world
To him who was wise
In a foolish world
To him who was just
In a base world
To him who was the weigher
And the measurer
The perfect appraiser
Of all the goods
And all the values
To him who in the labyrinth
Of my shifting days

Was a light at my feet
And a staff in my hand
To him—
My inimitable Companion
DISILLUSION!

CODICIL:

The rags
I bequethe
To the Eternal Survivor
King of all Kings
Master of the Earth
His Magnificence
WORM!

Great and Holy Kong-Fu-Tse
Fountain without end
Of Virtue and of Truth,
I salute you
And bid you
Farewell!

Lao She Recounts the Ironic Parable of the Log and the Trees

Thus did the ancient Log
Sapless and branchless
Save for one black arm
Protruding like a menacing horn
Of the embattled rhinoceros
Preach to the forest
In Spring:
"O Trees of the Earth
Harken!

Shake off your vain leaves
Break your proud boughs
Refuse to dance
To the passion-laden songs
Of the vagabond winds
Splash to the ground
The voluptuous moon
Scatter like rain drops
The frivolous birds!
Be not
Like the saucy-tongued grasses
Inconstant
Spread not
Like the wanton flowers
Maddening incense!
Harken
O Trees of the Earth,
Or the merciless ax
Of the Lord of the Forests
Lightning-edged
Shall strike you
And cleave you
And the thousand-tongued
God of Flames
Shall consume you
Unto ashes!
Harken!"

To a Mandarin Who Did Not Deign to Visit To Mi, Humble Poet

Seeing that you refused
To visit me,
O Perfect Prince,
The Morning Sun,
To console me,
Entered
Most reverentially
My tiny, ill-furnished room.

Ti Wung Lo Says That Illusion Is More Beautiful Than Reality

At the end of every feast
Famous for its prodigality
The melancholy Emperor
Sighed:
"More gorgeous are the banquets
Hungry beggars dream of."

Ki K'ang Sees His Own Fate in the Withered Leaves of His Garden

Withered leaves—
Clattering fragments
Of emerald cups
Once o'erbrimming
With the vintage
Primeval
Of the Sun.

Withered leaves—
Cramped ghosts
Of pulsing palms
On which birds danced
And the moon
Weary with vigil
Slept
In silver rainment.

Withered leaves—
Trailing shreds
Of glittering silk
Whereon laughing Summer
Wrote "Life"
And mournful Autumn
Writes "Death!"

Withered leaves—
Crumbling epitaphs
To my magic dreams
Of yesteryear.

Ti Tsung, Poet, Envisages the Future of Himself and His Sweetheart

You sit there huddled
Deep within your chair
Three-fourths of you hidden
One fourth guessed—
A bit of shoulder
The dim suggestion
Of a breast
A pair of toes
Peeping from within
The velvet sandals
Tips of fingers
Holding my poem
Its silk shimmering
A lake
Creased by the breeze.

So often have you sat there
And read my poems
So often have I watched you
And loved you
And owned you.

Alas!
Some strange to-morrow
Shall break upon us,
And I shall find
An empty chair
With fluttering images
And endless sorrow,
Or you shall sit alone
Deep within it
Your bosom still

Your eyes seeking
And on the floor
Crumpled
A face in anguish
My poem.

Ling Ma Answers His Friend Who Complains That Things Pass

The swift-footed River asks
Wrinkling his mighty brow:
"Why do shores fly past me
Forever
Like two giant gulls?"

Tchan Su's Unfinished Masterpiece

I was writing my final poem,
"The Wisdom of Life,"
When Li Hung's ghost
White and tremulous
Like a thin sun-beam
Upon a waterfall
Spoke to me
Through the open window:
"Has not Tchan Su learned yet
The Wisdom of Life?"
The moths are eating
The silken leaves
Of "The Wisdom of Life,"
While I am drinking
Countless cups of wine.

Wang Chang, the Mad Philosopher, Dismisses Himself

You are Man
Therefore my enemy—
My joys you covet
And barter them
For your pains—
My sorrows you despise
And proud the fates
Have favored you
You grin your pity
And pass me on.
You laugh with me
You cheer with me
You hail me brother—
I have no fear
For I have locked my door
And hid my love
And armored thrice my heart
Against your venomed shafts
Thrice coated
With the moulded honey
Of hypocrisy.

You are Man
Mask within mask
Sans number,
Vain clown
In a tumultuous fair
Turning somersaults
To vain applause—
My Enemy
MYSELF!

Mung Li Discovers the Meaning of Distance

Mung Li,
Prophet of the Perfect God,
Climbs the Tall Hill
To spit upon the City of Ugliness
And utter his malediction.
From the round peak
Of the Tall Hill
The City of Ugliness
Is a coronet of jade
Divinely fashioned.

Si Mo Ridicules Vainglory

The rusty weathercock
On Mi Po's humble roof
Turns drearily about itself
Creaking:
"I, Maker and Master of Tempests,
Have unreined the Thousand Steeds
Whose hoofbeats shake the Face of the Earth—
People of the Celestial Empire
Beware!"

Fan Ch'i in Search of Lost Time

It rains
My windows and my doors
Are barred
And I am alone—
Come now my dreams
Come as you came of yore
With the rays of the sun
In your eyes
And the fragrance of the fields
In your nostrils—
Come
Dance before me
Shod with the breezes
Of the summer—
Come
Sing to me
Throated with the songs of the birds.
Long have my doors and my windows
Been open
Long have my rooms
Echoed with the clamor
Of the street—
But now it rains
And my windows and my doors
Are barred
And I am alone,
Come
My dreams!
Your dreams have died
With the winds
Your dreams have passed
With the waters,
Time has devoured your dreams,
O Fan Ch'i!

Tching Wu, Lover of Mankind, Opens His Heart

Having locked and barred my doors
Most securely
I walk among people
Smiling serenely
Calling each one
"My dearest friend
My beloved brother."

The Mistress of the Son of Heaven Bewails Her Fate

At night
Before unrobing
The Mistress of the Son of Heaven
Gazing at herself
In the long mirror
Which glows
Like a fistful of diamonds
Sighs:
"The peacock can go to sleep
In her beautiful feathers."

Tung Si Explains the Meaning of Time and of Age

The lithesome kitten
Dashes after all things
With flaming eyes
And outstretched claws
Believing them timorous mice.
The horny tom-cat
His head between his paws
Blinks at moving things
Knowing they are but the trailing shadows
Of birds in flight.

Wun Chai Tsal Takes an Inventory

A crushed rose in a book
Whose leaves are yellow
A lock of faded hair
Tied with a red ribbon
Turned white
A pack of letters
Crumbling between fingers
A photograph scraped
By the nails of Time
Leaving but a dim suggestion
Of a girl's smile—
These—
And the memory
Of a perfumed breath
Upon the face
The pressure of a soft body
Against the chest
And the sudden flutter
Of a hummingbird
Upon the window-pane
A scared laugh
And a glow of pearls—
These—
And the pain
Of unassuaged hunger—
These—
And the agony of vain regrets—
These are the faded rags
Of my imperial love
These the crumbled dust
Of my immortal love—

Li Po's Plea to His Beloved

Do not tell me the truth—
I would not hear
That love must die
That raging fires pale
And turn to frozen ashes—
I would not learn
That lips must harden
Into stone
And chill the lips they touch
That the eye looks
But cannot see
That the breast presses
But the heart
Beneath it
Is still and mute.
Do not tell me the truth—
Tell me lies!
Tell me
That a kind divinity
Breathed into our love
Eternal life
And you and I are woven
Into a blazing star
Whose flames
Not all the mouths
Of all the centuries
Can blow out.
Tell me
That winds have not scattered
Our joys
With the withered leaves
And the dust of the lanes.
Tell me

That your hand
Still trembles
At the touch of my sleeve
That the sound of my steps
Approaching
Still raises your pulse
As the new moon raises
The tide of the sea.
Tell me
The multitudinous things
That were truth
Tell me
And I shall bury my head
In your breast
And perhaps as I hear you
I shall believe
And perhaps as you speak
By some sweet incantation
Your words shall seem
Truth even to you.
Tell me lies, O Beloved,
Do not tell me the truth!

Wong Lung Po Believes that Even as He Himself Is Sadly Aware of the Discrepancy Between His Dreams and His Accomplishments So Things in Nature Must Also Be

THE BREEZE:

In my dreams
I uproot forests
Tear mountains
From their anchors

Splash the grinning Moon
With the salt waters
Of the Seas
Sweep before me
Like weightless clouds
All things mighty and ponderous.

In truth
All I achieve
With my utmost force
Is raise fistfuls
Of vagrant dust
Dangle dying leaves and petals
Hold triumphant aloft
A moulting fledgling's feather
Waft to bees' eager nostrils
The urging scent
Of lecherous flowers
And serve as dainty fan
To cool a maiden's
Blushing cheek.

THE BUTTERFLY:

In my dreams
I am a majestic eagle
I spread colossal wings
Tear through iron clouds
Swoop to Earth
And capture with my dazzling talons
Bleating, shivering sheep.
My nest I perch
Upon the snowy crest
Of the Blue Mountain
Where I live forever.

In truth
I am a bit of gauze
Rocking on trembling petals
At the mercy of all the winds
Chased by impudent children
And madcap men.
I shall end my solitary day
In the dirt of the road
My velvet torn
And my colors washed
Or transfixed
My wings outspread
Mocking flight
Within a tomb of glass.

THE RAIN:

In my dreams
I am a celestial Ocean
Breaking cosmic dams
I hurl myself
Against the trembling Earth
I sink within her
I cover her
I drown her
I rise above her
Higher
Higher
Until the peaks
Of her measureless mountains
Are lost beneath me.

In truth
I am multitudinous threads
Of luke warm water
Spouting from the wombs
Of feathery clouds
Falling
Dizzily
To the ground—
I turn dust to mud
And make troughs
For birds to slake their thirst
And bugs to dart in.
The Sun laughs
And I vanish.

THE WORM:

In my dreams
I am a gigantic snake
My great mouth
A black cavern
Brimming with venom
My tongue a rapier
Dipped in flames
My eyes glowing suns
Dazing birds
Their song frozen
In their throats
Their wings
Drooped
Stiffened
Awaiting my embrace
Of Death.

In truth
I crawl
Warily
On barks of trees
And zig-zag
My perilous way
Through fields of grasses
Seeking putrid grub.
I shall end
Wriggling on a hook
Bait for foolish fish
Or from the beak
Of a sparrow
To be plunged
Into the gullet
Of her famished fledgling.

THE LAMB:

In my dreams
I am a man
I fleece sheep
And slash their throats
I quarter them
And broil them
Over sizzling flames
I devour
Delighted
The fragrant flesh
And throw the bones
To tail-wagging
Mastiffs.

In reality
I must pasture
In a rocky field
And tear the tasteless grass
From between the stones
The shepherd raps me
With his crook
And the dog
Bites my legs
Helpless
I shiver
And bleat
Meh-meh-meh-
And await
The shears
And the knife.

THE CAT:

In my dreams
I am a royal tiger
My coat dazzling
In the flaming sun
Of the Great Jungle—
With vast cunning
I move in stealth
And utter silence
As shadows move
Through thick swamps
And foliage
Tortuous and dense
And fling myself
Upon the shivering deer
Tear his throat
Drink the hot blood

And drag the carcass
To a shady cave—
My gullet brimming
With sweet water
I plunge my fangs
Through the hide
And fill my belly
With the luscious flesh.

In reality
I am an alley cat
Mangy and famished
Forever seeking
In cans of garbage
Foul bits
To soothe
My cramping guts
And dodging shrewdly
The filthy dogs
Whose barkings
Shatter me.
I am the Great Hunter
But the mice are dwelling
In the closets
And feed on luscious food—
In vain do I meaw and meaw
No door ever opens
To welcome me—
I am the alley cat
Chased by dog and by man
And mocked by mice.

THE LIZARD:

In my dreams
I am my Ancestor
The Terrible Dinosaur
I weigh more than mountains
And devour forests
My measureless tail
In sheer play
Uproots trees
And scoops rocks,
At the thunderous clanging
Of my vast armor
All creatures
Flee in terror—
I am Master of the Earth
Invincible
Immortal!

In reality
I am a puny degenerate
A miserable Lizard
Fearful of petty noises
And of trembling shadows
I crawl over stones
And hide within their crevices
I hunt blind ants
And wingless vermin—
And in utter degradation,
O Great Ancestor,
Our effigy serves
As base pins
To hold together rags.

MAN:

In my dreams
I am as the god
Who in playful mischief
Molded and shaped
From the drifting clouds
Stars and suns
And myriad earths
And hurled them
Athwart the Great Emptiness
And laughed
But me
He fashioned
From imperishable flesh
And gazing at himself
In the Mirror Lake
He carved every trait
In perfect semblance
"Man!"
He exclaimed triumphant
"Immortal!
Eternal!"
And the cosmos trembled
With the echo
"Man!
Immortal!
Eternal!"

In truth
I am as the braying ass
And the hissing snake
And the hooting owl
Kneaded
From corrupting offal
Blended

With the crumbling dust
And enduring
'Twixt the opened womb
And the sealed tomb
The hour the Earth
Whirls about the sun
In her drunken jig.
I kill
And tear
And crush
And in blazing madness
I turn all things
To ashes
And raise
Ever higher
The towering
Monument of Tears.

Young Prince Meng Hao-Jan, Wearied of Flattery and Court Intrigues, Sings the Song of Himself and Laments His Fate

Ah, to be lost
And forgotten
Ah, to be hated
And cast aside
Ah, to be untrammeled
Unyielding
Master of Me!
Ah, to be unyoked
Untombed
From Country and Court
A vagabond

Roaming the Earth
Unruled
As the tide
Untouched
As the grave
Lost
And forgotten
Master of Me!
Ah, to be unshackled
From tongues
Drooling
With honey
From knees
Bended
With bile
Lost
And forgotten
Master of Me!

Alas,
To-morrow
When my Father
Is poisoned
I shall become
Emperor
Of all Cathay!

Pei Cheng, Poet, Who Knows the Tongues of All Things, Overhears a Dialogue and Walks Away Much Saddened

WORM:

In Autumn
The headless stalk
Shakes mournfully.

ROSE-BUD:

Autumn is dead
Spring has stabbed him
With her silver sword.

WORM:

Who has told you,
Red Rose-Bud,
That Autumn is dead?

ROSE-BUD:

Prince Butterfly
Wisest of beings
Lord of all the flowers
Of the Great Garden.

WORM:

Has Prince Butterfly
Told you,
Red Rose-Bud,
About whiffs of dust,
Once royal wings,
Whistling Wind
Blows into the gutter?

ROSE-BUD:

Wind is no more,
Golden-mouthed Summer
Has wafted him
Far far away
There is only Breeze
His sweet breath
Fans my face.

WORM:

Red Rose-Bud,
Have you heard
About white-ribbed Snow
Who freezes the heart?

ROSE-BUD:

Golden-eyed Summer
Has melted Snow
Into warm Rain
Who washes my face.

WORM:

Has Prince Butterfly,
Red Rose-Bud,
Spoken to you
About Master Worm
And his deeds?

ROSE-BUD:

He crawls
And the Great Garden
Is very big.

WORM:

It is true
He crawls
And the Great Garden
Is very big—
But
He always
Arrives
On time.

Yen Yuen's Dilemma

Last Summer
I vowed that love
Is eternal as the Stars
As constant as the Moon
That kisses the pouting mouths
Of the Waters,
But Liu Chin-Hsun, my sweetheart,
Laughed
And whispered into my ear:
"The scarlet rose, Yen Yuen,
Dies with the night,
The song of the nightingale
Vanishes with the passing wind
Love is like the scarlet rose
Love is like the song of the nightingale."

Now
I speak of love
That like the scarlet rose
Dies with the night
That like the song of the nightingale

Vanishes with the passing wind,
But Hung Sin-Mi, my sweetheart,
Buries her wet face
Into my chest
And whispers:
"Yen Yuen, are not the Stars eternal
Does not the Moon always
Kiss the pouting mouths
Of the Waters?
Love is like the Stars
Love is like the Moon."

Yuen Jang Discovers the Cure for His Ills

Though the Fates are the Masters
And the winds drag me
Whither they list
Companion of the smoke
And the stiffened leaf
Though born of a jest
At the dawn of a day
And dead of a pain
At its dusk
I am unconquered
And unconquerable
For I can laugh!
When Life mocks me
I answer her a merrier tune
When she orders
"Weep for my Law
Is the Law of Sorrows!"
I bend upon myself
And laugh.
When with anger maddened

She strikes my face
I reel and fall
But through the dust
And the tears
And the blood
My throat shakes
And I laugh!
I have gauged the tricks of the gods
I have seen the depth and the hearts of things
And I laugh
And laugh
And laugh
Until the winds roll with the echo
And the white-eyed Moon
Shakes behind the clouds.

I am unconquered
I am unconquerable
I, the Laugher!

Tsang Wam, Priest of the Summit Temple, Watches the Procession

The procession passes
On and on
From abysmal Nowhere
To abysmal Nowhere
Insistent
Even-stepped
And the one-toned lamentations
Fill the hollow winds
While Emperor Death
Rides triumphant
On his black horse.

Silent are the rising
And the setting Sun
And silent the Stars
And the white-eyed Moon
And in the distance
Glares a silent God.

The procession passes
On and on
From abysmal Nowhere
To abysmal Nowhere
Insistent
Even-stepped
While Gotama,
The Enlightened One,
Nirvana attained
His legs crossed
And his hands folded
Gazes at his navel
The center of the Universe.

Leong Koa-Trion, Courtier, and His Soul

At dawn
From the bottomless profundities
Of his majestic Self
Leong Koa-Trion, Courtier,
Plucked
With the most delicate care
His soul
His exquisite
Incomparable
Immortal
Soul.

He placed him
With gravest reverence
Upon a tall pedestal
Of dazzling jade
And bowing thrice
With imperial dignity
Exclaimed:
"O my Soul
My exquisite
Incomparable
Immortal
Soul!"

At twilight
Leong Koa-Trion's Soul
Mounted
A golden Butterfly
Which had fluttered
In scandalous intimacy
About his lips
And vanished
Sans adieu
And sans compunction
By the open window
Of the royal mansion.

Now
Leong Koa-Trion, Courtier,
Has no more Soul
No exquisite
Incomparable
Immortal Soul.

Now
He is an empty
Perpendicular drum
For all who will
To beat their sticks upon.

Nan-Kung Kwoh's Ultimate Posture

Once—
Within a field of redolent clover
And grasses soft as velvet tongues
I raised with tenderest solicitude
Illusions—
Countless perfect lambs
With fleece of silk
And eyes of honey—
But I wearied
Of their bleating
Mellifluous
As the murmuring waters
Of hidden brooks—
I slashed their trusting throats
And cast their carcasses
To the laughing hyenas
Of Reality.

Later—
In cages of ancient jade
Studded with imperial gems
I raised with punctilious care
Ironies—
Swarms of giant wasps
With scarlet legs
And black beaks
Sharp as surgeons' needles—
But I wearied
Of the clatter
Of their amber wings
Abstruse and intricate
As litanies of insane monks—
I pierced their bellies

Strung them on barbed wire
And fashioned
The thornèd crown
Of Truth.

Now—
In the dust and dung of the Road
Legs crossed and belly naked
I sit
A Buddha
Freed of Reality
Relieved of Truth
My emptiness merging
With the emptiness
Of the Cosmos.

Master Tsang Sin Warns His Pupils Against Boastfulness

His wings were white
As snow
His bill was black
As night
He could stand on one leg
And foretell the rain
Throw his head back
And uphold the moon
Paddle in the puddle
More smoothly than a leaf
Dash across the yard
Scare the cackling hens
And the howling dog
And what worm red or white

Could hide deeply enough
Within mud or dung
To escape his mighty claws?
Never had there been
So astonishing a drake
In yard or coop
Since ducks laid eggs
And drakes laid ducks!
And this he quacked
And quacked
And quacked
From dawn to dusk
That all the world might hear
Quack!
Quack!
Until one day
Annoyed by the clamor
His master
Grabbed him by the legs
Placed his neck
Throbbing with quacks
Upon a log
And with one thrust
Of the cleaver
Severed it. . .
And life went on
And ducks laid eggs
And drakes laid ducks. . . .

Kin Wan Watches His Reflection

Turn
Brown Mouse
Dizzily
In broken circles
Within your trap
That I may see
How I turn
Dizzily
In broken circles
Within my own,
Bruise your flanks
Against the spikes
Which imprison you
That I may feel
The barbs of envy
And of hate
Which pierce
And shackle me,
Shiver
Brown Mouse
And cower at my gaze
That I may quail
At my shadow
Staring
Stonily
From the mirror,
Bare your teeth
Sharp and glowing
Chips of pearls
Studded in red plush,
Bite the wire
Try to bend it
With your claws

Shrivelled twigs
Which crack and break
Beneath the weight of birds,
That I may witness
My frantic gestures
My raging antics
My ludicrous challenge
To my Evil Fate.
When I drown you,
Brown Mouse
Gasp and rap
Your quivering body
Against the water
That I may know
How I shall gasp
And toss
My fevered head
Against the burning sea
Of my pillow.
And when at last
Stiff and bloated
Your eyes bleeding
And your mouth cracked
You float in peace
You will not be
A dead Mouse
A murdered Beast
But the sum total
The ultimate meaning
Of Myself.

Koo-Sow, Celebrated Mathematician, Achieves the Perfect Conclusion

Each year in passing
Offered me its final gift—
A dead hope
A shattered illusion
A friend turned foe
A buried love
A dimmed eye
An ear frozen into stone
Subtle pains
That knew no relief
A fistful of teeth
A hairless skull
A bent back
A skin wrinkled
Like a pond
Into which a rock is cast
And frail as a page
Written by a scholar
During a dynasty long forgotten.
I plumbed
The deepest wells of numbers
I wandered
Through the dark labyrinths
Of intricate calculations
To fathom the meaning
And the purpose
Of the years of my life—
At last I triumphed
I solved the impenetrable riddle:
LIFE EQUALS ZERO
The vast circular Emptiness
Through which like wild steeds

At a circus
The years dash
And vanish
In the measureless abyss
Of Nothingness.

Now I sit upon the threshold
Of my humble home
And drink my cup of wine
And wait,
Unconcerned
Unperturbed
For the last wild steed
To dash through the circle
Of Emptiness.

To Fung Speaks of the Hazards of Kindness

One day
Wung Ghen's tamed fox
Found more delicious
The hand of his master
Than the meat
He offered him.

Lin Piao, Deposed Governor, Replies to those Who Claim that a True Mandarin Should Suffer Without Complaining

The tongueless fish
Is silent
Though he be sliced
Into tiny bits—
Is he the magnificent Monarch
Of all creation?

Thich-Nhat Blames the Evil Conditions of Cathay That Pigmies Appear as Giants

In my dark cellar
The smoke-tipped flame
Of the stinking
Sputtering
Tallow candle
Blinds like the sun
Perched upon the peak
Of the Blue Mountain.

Lung Mi Laughs at Those Who Try to Understand Themselves

Anxious to capture his dream
Fung-Su remained awake
The whole night.

Tsz-Lu Rejects the Yoke

No!
Not eternal love, O Lang-Ping!
Why should we learn
How soon the dregs
Are reached?
One deep draught
Of the cup
Filled with the wine
Of the Sun
And the milk
Of the moon—
And let us part!

Twang Ti's Prayer

I am a deep valley
And my love a high hill,
O mighty Wind,
Master of All Things,
Crumble her
That she may lie with me!

Chu Chiminh Is Fearful of the Fate of His Hopes

My hopes
Are gay-painted moths
Fluttering deliriously
But red-eyed Flame
Whistles . . .

My hopes
Are madcap robins
Singing rapturously
But green-eyed Cat
Watches . . .

My hopes
Are silver-toed rays
Dancing on the waters
But black-eyed Night
Swallows . . .

My hopes
Alas!
My hopes . . .

Pih Hih Complains Against Time

Ah, Time,
You are a whore—
For every pleasure you afford me
For every gesture that delights
You stretch your cupped hands
And demand them filled
Until you blaze
With all my bartered possessions.
When I must place
Upon your greedy finger-tips
My ultimate pulse
Vague and trembling
You will turn
In uttermost contempt
Your glowing back
And let me rot

Forever
In the coarse embrace of mud
And in the slimy mouths
Of worms.
Ah, Time,
You are a whore!

Po Li Compliments His Beloved

Even if the moon burned out
Like a neglected candle
Offered at the altar
Of forgotten ancestors
And her last flicker
Shivered and died
In the voracious mouth
Of Time,
I would remember her
Always
By the whiteness
And the roundness
Of your breasts,
O beloved Ho-Tsu-Ching!

Fan Hué, the Prophet, Foretells Earth's Ultimate Fate

The Mice
The inhabitants of the Earth
The cosmic Cellar
Are gnawing clamorously

And disturb
The sleeping stars—
The Ancient Guardian
Swings his lantern,
The White Moon,
As he descends
The mouldy steps
Of Infinity
While the Black Cat
Under his arms
Meaws
Impatiently.

Chi Yi, Deposed General, Bewails the Irony of His Fate

The grey sparrow
Dashes across the fields
With chirps of triumph,
While in the cage
His great wings outspread
His eyes glowing
The mighty eagle
Dashes his head
Against the bars.

Kung-Shu Wan Ridicules Flattering Courtiers

Yuen Sz's soul
Bent so low
And so often
It turned

At last
Upon itself
And became
A perfect hoop
Which any hand
Could roll
Wherever it listed.

Liu Chao-Chi Chides a Vociferous Rebel Against Society

The grain of sand
White with the foam
Of the morning tide
Grits defiance:
"I am I!
I shall not let
Millions of grains
Press against me
Stifle me
Make me
An indistinguishable part
Of the monstrous
Shapeless
Shore!
I am I!
I challenge the winds
I challenge the waters
I challenge the millions of grains
That form
The monstrous
Shapeless
Shore!
I am I!"

Fan Chi Explains the Millennium

Dandelions
Golden-headed
Silver-winged
Blossoming
On the bosom of the snow.

Sin Tchu Is Perplexed

Why do my hopes
Yellow, withered leaves,
Drop to the ground
And mingle with the mud,
While my regrets,
Giant evergreens,
Cast their black shadows
Across my path?

Tsz-Chang Warns That People Do Not Really Change

The wind blows—
The same clouds
Roll and break
Assuming many shapes.

A Novel in Twelve Poems

I

MUNG LUNG WARNS A GIRL, WHO OVERPROUD OF HER YOUTH, REJECTS HIM

You balance upon your head
With superb assurance
A crystal vase,
But Time,
O Cherry Blossom,
Is an arrow
Well-aimed.

II

CHERRY BLOSSOM ANSWERS MUNG LUNG, MOCKING HIS AGE

Words,
O Mung Lung,
Are formidable shadows
Tiny objects cast
When Time,
The Giant Candle,
Is behind them
Flickering in the wind.

III

A YEAR LATER—CHERRY BLOSSOM COMPLAINS AGAINST LO MI, HER SEDUCER

I thought it was soft Night
Embracing me.
I closed my eyes
And slept . . .
It was the thick black shadow
Of the hawk.

IV

LO MI REPLIES TO CHERRY BLOSSOM

I said my love was a flower
An exquisite rose
And you were happy—
Do not flowers wither in the Autumn?
Do not roses scatter their petals?
Why do you weep?

V

CHERRY BLOSSOM INFORMS MUNG LUNG OF HER SORROW

The crystal vase
Lies shattered
Like a million grains of sand.
My head,
O Mung Lung,
Is tightened between my palms.

VI

MUNG LUNG RENEWS HIS PROPOSAL

The grains of sand,
O gentle Cherry Blossom,
Are precious jewels
In the setting Sun.

VII

CHERRY BLOSSOM ACCEPTS

I am blowing the sand,
O Mung Lung,
Toward the West,
That it may reach
Much sooner
The tender rays
Of the setting Sun.

VIII

TWO MONTHS LATER: CHERRY BLOSSOM, TIRED OF MUNG LUNG, RUNS AWAY

Night,
The Black Serpent,
Has swallowed the Scarlet Bird—
The rising Sun,
O Mung Lung,
Is a silver Wing.

IX

MUNG LUNG TELLS HIS FRIEND, KUNG TCHI, THAT HE INTENDS TO COMMIT SUICIDE

Nothing is left me now
Save an armful of ashes—
Blow upon them
O passing Wind!

X

KUNG TCHI COUNSELS MUNG LUNG TO DESIST FROM HIS DECISION

Thus, O desperate Mung Lung,
Spoke the Ancient Tree
To the leaf that was weary of him:
"It is far better for a leaf
To hang upon its branch
Though it be eaten by many worms
And dangled by all the winds
Like a broken cord,
For the leaf that has dropped to the Earth
Be it greener than the heart of Spring
And smoother than the face of the Moon
Is crushed by hoofs
And mingled with the dust."

XI

SOME YEARS LATER: CHERRY BLOSSOM WRITES TO MUNG LUNG THAT SHE IS DYING AND BEGS FORGIVENESS

The silver Wing,
O Mung Lung,
Is beating the dust,
How weakly,
Alas!
Does the bird
Forgive the arrow
That pierced it?

XII

MUNG LUNG BEING LONG DEAD, KUNG TCHI, HIS FRIEND, REPLIES TO CHERRY BLOSSOM

Over the Cataract
Eternity
All shadows fall
And mingle.

Min Tsz-Kien, Archivist of the Great and the Little Cemeteries, Discovers the Wills of Some of the Occupants and Adds His Commentaries—

I

You were buried,
Ki K'ang,
As you desired
Beneath the ancient elm
Whose cool black shadow
Lay upon your grave
As a knightly armor
Guarding you against

The Sun's blazing arrows.
Last Autumn
Lightning struck it
And cleaved it
And the dead wood
Fed neighboring fires.
It is Summer now once again—
Are your eyes,
Ki K'ung,
Blinded
By the Sun's blazing arrows?

II

For your immortal memory
As you willed it,
Fei Huang,
The bronze fountain was erected
In the City Square,
And upon it was carved
The verse you composed:
"Drink, gentle asses, and refresh yourselves"—
But asses no longer pass the City Square
The water no longer runs
The bronze is devoured
By the red fangs of rust
And the people laugh
"Fei Huang the fool!
Throw the fountain into the River
And wipe his name forever
From the memory of Man!"
Mourn not,
Good Fei Huang,
The perversity of Time
And the insolence of Man!
Sleep in peace in your grave

Buried beneath the tall weeds,
Be the perfect host to worms
As you were to asses!

III

Your tombstone,
Nan Yung,
For which you spent
All your wealth
Disinheriting your heirs,
Is the tallest
Of the Great Cemetery
And its marble dazzles
As a midday Sun
Amid pallid Moons—
Do the Guardian Spirits
As they pass
In their nightly watch
Bow reverently before it
And like somber winds
Whistling through narrow alleys
Hail you:
"O great Nan Yung,
May the worms spare you
May the rains cleanse you
May your bones glow
Like the imperishable marble
Of your majestic tombstone!"

IV

Your tombstone
Is a thin yellow slab
Shaking in the wind
Like an old man's last tooth
His tongue striking it

As he speaks—
Nothing is legible on it
Save the brave words
You flung at the scornful face
Of despicable Destiny:
"I AM MASTER!"
O Nameless One,
Has Destiny crawled before you
As a dog whose hind legs are broken
And whined:
"Forgive, O Great Lord,
The outrageous tricks
I played upon you,
And accept me,
I implore you,
As your humble and repentant
Slave?"

V

In Life,
Wang Chang,
You were as one dead
Disdained and ridiculed
And the many words
Which you drew
With such care and diligence
Upon the shimmering silk
Had less merit
Than the barking of a stray dog
Fearful of the reflection
The Moon waves
Among dry noisy leaves.
In Death,
You are as one living
Honored and esteemed—

"Wang Chang is as wise
As Kong-Fu-Tse
And his verses
Are as skillful
As those of the Shi-King."
From far-away provinces
Come old and young
To place flowers upon your tomb,
They bow their heads
And pronounce your name
In reverence.
Does it please you,
Wang Chang?
Does it enrage you,
Wang Chang?

VI

"I cast a net
Into the White River
And caught many fish,
But a craftier Angler
Cast *his* net
And caught me
And dragged me
Into the Earth.
Beware,
Passers-by,
Lest you, too,
Be trapped
Into his net!"
This,
Pih-le He,
You willed to be carved
On your tombstone.
Alas,

Your disrespectful heirs
Squandered your money
And carved upon a frail slab
"Pih-le-He—
Fisherman."
No Passer-by
Stops before it
And the wild grasses
Are smothering it—
Does it matter,
Pih-le He?

VII

Your heirs
Obeyed your whim
And raised two tombstones
On two graves for you.
On one they carved
As you desired:
"Here lies
Kung-ming Kaou
As he was
But would not be."
On the other:
"Here lies
Kung-ming Kaou
As he was not
But would be."
Ah, Kung-ming Kaou,
The tombstones are buried
Face down in the mud
Their words erased,
The full coffin
And the empty one
Were carried off

By the flood
And lie in a heap
Beneath a mound of manure—
Yet, peace!
Some dawn
On its crest
The cock will flap his regal wings
And trumpet to the world
Majestically
The advent of the Sun
And the unification
Of the two Kung-ming Kaou!

VIII

Your tombstone
Wrought with consummate skill
T'ai-Pih, Master Sculptor,
Is a precious legacy
And your words carved into it
Polished by knife and file
Shimmer in the Moonlight
Like crawling Serpents' scales:
"Man's Life is Evil—
His mouth a gargoyle
Through which pour foul lies,
His hand a wild claw
Ripping the throat
Of fellow-man,
His heart a cauldron
Boiling with greed and envy,
His brain a mound of dung
Over which buzz the vicious Flies
Of Ignorance and Superstition—
The Earth groans
Beneath his arrogant spiked feet."

O Master T'ai-Pih,
Is Man's *Death* Good?
Is his locked mouth
A treasury of truth?
His crooked hand
A gesture of benediction?
His frozen heart
A well of Love and Compassion?
His stony brain
A redolent forest
Within which scintillate
The iridescent worms of Wisdom and Knowledge?
Does the Earth sing
As she feels the tender pressure
Of his bony heels?
And Master T'ai-Pih,
When Man has merged into the Universal Body
As a stream merged into the Sea
Forever drowned in its salt,
Is it Evil?
Is it Good?

IX

"My days were waves
Of the Sea of Evil
Hurling against me—
Pain and Sorrow
A faithless Wife
And vicious Sons—
I labored hard and long
But all in vain
And the Gods as recompense
Gave me Death—
Is this mockery justice?"

Your complaint
Deeply carved
Into your tombstone
That it may never be erased,
Nan-Kung,
Is an irreverent wind
Clamping the nostrils with stench
And blinding the eyes with dust.
The Gods in their infinite innocence
Know not the meaning of justice
And their perpetual somnolent tranquillity
Is not the temper for mockery.
Leave the Gods alone,
Nan-Kung,
The Earth is not their habitation
And Man in his boundless vanity
Is not their concern
They know him not.
Let him who reasons
Carve into his tombstone
The eternal Truth of Life and Death:
"I was not—
I was—
I am not."

X

"Let there be Peace!"
These were your last words
The ultimate essence
Of your superior wisdom,
O renowned Mang-tsze,
Chiselled into the Stone
Like an Imperial Decree
For all to read
And all to obey.

And all read
And all obeyed
And Princes and Kings and Generals
Within the Great Wall
Warred against one another
And flooded our vast Empire
With cataracts of blood.
"Let there be Peace!"
All trumpted loftily,
But each would bring it
To the others
By fire and sword and famine,
For Peace springs from the loins of War
But the loins were sterile
And no Peace was born.
Ah, wise Mang-tsze,
Ah, good Mang-tsze,
If your eyes were not hollowed
And crawling with worms
They would pour such wild tears
Of utter grief
To overflow the fathomless
Well of Bitter Sorrows.

XI

"I was the mistress
Of illustrious men,
My lap was laden
With precious gifts,
I was loved and feted
But I was unhappy
For I did not pursue
The Good Way
And did not obey
The Rules of Propriety—

O Women of Cathay
Be poor and lonely
But remain virtuous
And you shall be happy."
And the virtuous women
Beaten by husbands
And derided by sons
Pelted the dazzling tombstone
With rocks and manure
And when it lay face down
They drowned it with their water.
"How dare you teach us morals
Sow without shame?
What price virtue
If we go hungry and ragged
And our homes are ratholes?
What meaning happiness
If there is no peace?
Brazen bitch
Rot on!"
No celebrated lover,
Lady Yang Kuei-fei,
Who filled your lap
With gold and gems
Or painted on choicest silk
Enraptured poetry
To your beauty and charms
Or hunted savage beasts
To place their skins
Beneath your tiny feet
Has come to lift your tombstone
From the stinking dung
And let it glow again
In the Milk of the Moon—
Do you weep,

Lady Yang Kuei-fei?
Do you laugh?
Do you shrug your bony shoulders
Once covered with skin
Smoother than velvet
And more fragrant than roses
Imprinted with the kisses
Of hungry mouths?

XII

"To know Myself
I relinquished
Love and Home
Fortune and honors
I studied the masterpieces
Of all the great Sages—
Days and nights
I meditated upon them
Until my hair turned white
And my eyes dimmed—
And as I lay
Awaiting the cool hand of Death
To soothe my burning brow
I suddenly achieved my mission!
I knew Myself—
I was NOBODY."
The Sages misguided you,
Sir Nobody,
To know yourself
Is gathering shadows
In the forests
And capturing echoes
In the deserts,
To know yourself
Is to destroy yourself—

You should have harkened
To your instinct,
Sir Nobody,
Which orders:
"Deceive yourself!
Accept the image
Of your deception!"
Thus you would have prospered
And your name glorified in History
Would have glowed
On your tombstone.

XIII

"I am Tsz-hia
I was Governor of Ku-Fu
I defeated invaders
I hanged robbers
I imprisoned vagabonds
I distributed rice
During the Long Famine
And the High Flood—
I forced the young
To do homage to the old
And all to revere
Ancestors and Sages—
My region knew security
And contentment—
I was your Benefactor,
Peoplc of Ku-Fu,
Forget me never!"
Alas, Governor Tsz-hia,
That the deeds of benefaction
Should weave a breastplate of gossamer
Torn by the Arrows of Time
While the weighty armor

Wrought of the steel of cruelty
And the brass of disdain
Should remain undented!
You are forgotten,
Governor Tsz-hia,
The people you ruled over
Are rotting bones
Even as yourself
And bones have no memories—
To forget and be forgotten
This is the meaning of Peace,
Governor Tsz-hia,
Sleep in Peace!

XIV

"Presume not,
Passer-by,
To read my inscription
Without bowing
Ceremoniously—
I am Duke Nagai,
General without Peer
Killer of countless thousands—
Weep not,
Silly fool,
Laugh not,
Vulgar knave,
My mighty Sword
Shall split you in two!"
Be not wroth
Duke Nagai,
He who reads the inscription
On your tombstone
Neither weeps
Nor laughs

Only shrugs—
One fears not a mighty sword
When the mighty hand which swayed it
Is rotting in the earth—
As for generals without peer
Who kill countless thousands
Their number is legion,
Duke Nagai,
And the water that runs in the gutter
Mingling with mud and ordure
Is more precious
Than the blood of men.

XV

"O wicked Death,
Why have you robbed me
Of my darling Fei?
A more beautiful child
The world has never seen,
The new-born lamb
Hopping after his mother
Was not more innocent,
The song of the birds
Was harsh as Autumn wind
Compared to his voice,
The sun was a candle light
Compared to his radiant smile—
Were there not in the world
O cruel Death,
Enough for your gorging:
The old, the crippled, the ugly?
Curse,
Passer-by
The Monstrous Ogre!"
Death was not wicked,

Overwrought Mother,
He loved your Fei
With a greater love than yours
And would not let him
Be mocked and mutilated
By the fierce claws of Time—
Body shrivelled
Skin turned leather
Mouth drooped
Eyes dimmed
Unworthy to compete
With the flickering light
Of the humble firefly
Darting over the swamp—
Rejoice,
Mother of Fei,
Your heart shall ever be filled
With untarnished beauty.

Curse not Death,
Passer-by
His merciful hands
Shall lift
The grievous burdens
Life, the Maleficent Master,
Is lading upon your back
Without reprieve—
In his arms folded
You shall sleep undisturbed.

XVI

"My music tamed
Warring kings
And haughty queens,
And wild beasts

Forgot claw and fang
While, unafraid,
Little creatures
Gamboled between their legs.
But one there was
I could not tame—
He scorned my work
He mocked my honors
He called me imposter
And cringing mountebank—
Squatting within me
Rooted in my bowels
He proclaimed himself
The true Yuen Jang—
Who lies here,
He or I?"
You both lie here
The true and the false,
And a thousand more
All your ancestors
Gathered in the dust.
You were but a link,
Master Yuen Jang,
In an unfinished chain
And they who preceded you
Clamored for attention
As you rode in hollow triumph
On the Tall Charger
Whose silver hooves
Scatter sparks
And whose ruby culus
Trumpets storms
On the stony Road to Nowhere.
But all is well now,
Master Yuen Jang,

Your chain is complete
And you have the sweet peace
Of Mother Dust.

XVII

"I was Ku Pih-yuh
Soldier in the Emperor's army
I left my wife in tears
And my children huddled in terror
To fight the Great War—
I was faithful and courageous
I did my solemn duty
Most honorably,
I killed many enemies
Before the fateful knife
Was plunged into my belly.
Did we win?
Is the Emperor safe?"
The Emperor is in his palace
On the golden throne
Surrounded by crafty courtiers
Watching the Dance of the Maids—
The country is governed
By arrogant avaricious overlords
New enemies are ramming the Wall
And fresh troops are recruited
For the New Great War—
Widows are weeping
Orphans are roaming the streets
The rich are fat
The poor are hungry
All is as it was
From the beginning of Time—
We won,
Brave Ku Pih-huy—

XVIII

"Disciples from the four corners
Of our vast Empire
Sat at my feet
And in reverence imbibed
My wisdom and my knowledge
And all said:
Behold Master Kung Che-ke
Of men the most learned
He knows everything!
And I walked the Earth
In majestic pride.
Humbly I beg now
Carve upon a plain tombstone:
Here is Kung Che-ke
All he taught were lies
He knew but one thing more
Than the rest of men—
He knew he knew nothing!
Forgive the imposter!"
And all say:
"How modest is Master Kung Che-ke
Among mortals without peer!
We understand the subtle meaning
Of your final words
O Pattern of Perfection,
And in reverence
We shall pursuc your teachings
And obey your precepts
Generation upon generation!"
In the Great Labyrinth
Of Perpetual Night
Wherein mankind wanders
Without issue
Lies are the lighted torches

And Truth is the evil Wind
Which blows them out.
Be of good cheer
Dust of Master Kung Che-ke
Mighty Torch-lighter
Your name shall blaze on
Forever!

XIX

"I am Han Suyin
Wife of Tan-choo—
Poets wrote about our love
And held us as models
For all to follow—
Tan-choo, my husband,
My Spirit shall wait for yours
At the gate of Heaven
As I always waited
On the doorstep of our home
For your return at night
Trembling with joy and anxiety.
Nevermore shall we be parted
We shall be immortal."
What is a Spirit,
Good Han Suyin,
But shapeless air
Without mouth to kiss
And arms to embrace?
And what is Heaven
But a vast Emptiness
Surrounded by a myriad
Blazing stars?
Tan-choo, your husband,
Did not long survive
And rests now beside you.

On his tombstone
He had carved only:
"I have come home,
Beloved Han Suyin."
Slowly the good Earth
Unites you both
In her motherly embrace.
You shall never be parted
And you shall be immortal
For lovers in all the Empire
Pray to all the gods:
"Grant us, we implore,
That we shall ever be
Like Han Suyin
And Tan-choo!"

XX

"I am Kung-ming Kaou,
Scholar and traveler,
I had houses and gardens
Wife and children
And many honors—
At the age of eighty
I was locked in a wooden box
And lowered into the earth—
What is the meaning of this?
What is the significance?
What is the ultimate purpose?"
The meaning,
Master Kung-ming Kaou,
Is that you lived
For eighty times the Earth
Spinned around the Sun,
And died.
The world does not tolerate

Corpses strewn about
And you were buried.
There is no significance
And there is no purpose
Neither immediate
Nor ultimate—
The circle is complete
The circumference obliterated
Time is drowned in Eternity—
Your cold bones,
Master Kung-ming Kaou,
Are turning into water
And mingle with the rains—
Farewell!

To Emperor Shun, Son of Heaven, His Eternal Servant Min Tsz-Kien, Archivist

Having read most carefully
The inscriptions on the tombstones
Of the Great and Little Cemeteries
I have the honor to suggest
To Your Imperial Majesty
The sole means of improving
The ways of the citizens of Cathay:
BURY ALL THE LIVING
AND RESURRECT THE DEAD!

E N D

Y U N